1,001
Pearls of
Bible Wisdom

1,001
Pearls of
Bible Wisdom

Malcolm Day

Insights and Inspirations from the Biblical Tradition

CHRONICLE BOOKS
SAN FRANCISCO

1,001 Pearls of Bible Wisdom
Malcolm Day

First published in the United States in 2008 by
Chronicle Books LLC.

First published in the United Kingdom and
Ireland in 2008 by Duncan Baird Publishers Ltd.,
Sixth Floor, Castle House, 75–76 Wells Street,
London W1T 3QH.

Library of Congress Cataloging-in-Publication
Data Available.

ISBN: 978-08118-6420-6

Printed in Thailand by Imago

Conceived, created and designed by
Duncan Baird Publishers.

Editor: Diana Loxley
Designer: Justin Ford
Managing Editor: Christopher Westhorp
Managing Designer: Daniel Sturges
Commissioned artwork: Jenny Reynish

Typeset in AT Shannon
Color reproduction by Scanhouse, Malaysia

10 9 8 7 6 5 4 3 2 1

Chronicle Books
680 Second Street
San Francisco, CA 94107

www.chroniclebooks.com

Note about Bible quotes

CONTENTS

Introduction   6

The Divine   12

In the Beginning   14

Mystic Communion   34

Heaven   52

Angels   68

The Word   85

Grace   94

Virtues   106

The Commandments   108

Love & Kindness   118

Wisdom & Truth   129

Forgiveness & Reconciliation   138

Repentance & Confession   146

Patience & Endurance   157

Humility   163

Courage & Fortitude	172
Duty	183
Prudence	190

| **Faith & Hope** | **198** |

Messages of the Prophets	200
The Ministry of Jesus	209
Teachings on Faith	217
Prayer	227
Miracles	239
Inspiration	249
Doubt	255
Freedom	263

| **Family Life** | **272** |

Hearth & Home	274
Procreation & Birth	282
Marriage	292

| Sons & Daughters | 302 |
| Posterity | 311 |

| **Friends & Neighbors** | **318** |

Friendship	318
Neighborhood	326
Working Together	339
Travel	350
Peace	361

Further Reading	374
Index	376
Acknowledgments	382

INTRODUCTION

All of us, at some point in our lives, need to look outside ourselves to gather strength when we feel weak, to find comfort in times of sorrow, courage in times of fear, peace in times of turmoil. Sometimes we may simply seek inspiration or enlightenment or want to develop a more positive attitude toward life. The "pearls" of wisdom presented in this book respond to needs such as these. They offer insights into thought-provoking themes and reflections on life's mysteries, some providing unexpected slants on familiar topics, others bringing clarity to complex issues. But all, in one way or another, are inspiring nuggets of wisdom from the Christian faith, notable for their beauty, brilliance, or insight.

Believers and non-believers alike recognize the Bible as a work of great depth and tremendous spiritual guidance, overflowing with remarkable characters and events, and containing some of the most gripping stories and beautiful poetry and prose ever written. Our anthology taps into this immense inspirational reservoir, drawing quotations from the Bible itself as well as from Christian writers and literature inspired by the Christian tradition—from letters, memoirs, and treatises to poetry and sometimes even fiction. If you are not a regular reader of the Bible, and even if you are, this book, with its hand-picked pearls of wisdom, will remind you of the wealth of inspirational sayings and proverbs it contains. It will also reveal how Christian thinkers through the ages have benefited from their study of the sacred book and passed on the gems of their reflection. As Job tells us, "It is not the old that are wise, nor the aged that understand what is right" (Job 32:9).

1,001 Pearls of Bible Wisdom is a collection to be dipped into at any spare moment, on topics ranging from courage, doubt, and forgiveness, to love, marriage, and angels, touching on such essential issues as day-to-day living and interaction with friends and neighbors. A fresh look at a common theme can often spring surprises: sibling rivalry, for example, is an age-old source of friction in the home, yet the biblical story of Joseph and his brothers shows that good can sometimes emerge from it.

The book is divided according to central aspects of Christian life and belief: from divinity, virtue, and morality, to faith and hope, family values, and issues surrounding personal and social relationships. Influential Christian thinkers, ancient and modern, contribute insights into faith and the human condition. Thus St. Augustine (354–430), after leading a life of dissolution, suggests that unless humility accompanies good deeds, "pride will snatch everything right out of our hands." Meanwhile the Spanish mystic St. Teresa of Avila (1515–1582) observes that "humility must always be doing its work like a bee making its honey in the hive."

Alongside the mighty minds of the Christian faith are those who have risen to prominence as a result of their actions in the world. The nurse Florence Nightingale (1820–1910), for example, dedicated her life to tending to wounded soldiers during the Crimean War—experiences that inspired her reading of scripture and became crystallized in her diary. One of her entries reflects on communion with God: "When we speak with God, our power of addressing him, of holding communion with him, and listening to his still small voice, depends on our will being one and the same with his." Many public figures in the modern era quote Christians who have expressed with beauty or insight the essence of what they wish to communicate. One example is the prayer of St. Francis of Assisi (c. 1182–1226), who yearned to bring peace wherever he went, so that "where there is hatred, I may bring love … where there is despair, I may bring hope … where there is sadness, I may bring joy."

Many of the quotations in the book stand alone, coming direct from the biblical or original source to the page, without supplementary context. In others, brief context has been added to help the reader reap the full benefit of the message. Some entries (for example, on the Annunciation, the Nativity, Feeding the Five Thousand, the Last Supper, the Good Samaritan, the Exodus) illuminate key concepts of the Christian faith—these

are presented in larger type so that they can easily be distinguished. In each case, the text summarizes the event and draws the reader's attention to its context and meaning. All biblical quotes are taken from the New Revised Standard Version (NRSV), unless otherwise indicated in parentheses by the initials "KJV" (King James Version).

From the many elements of the Christian gospel spring the thoughts of two thousand years of Christian thinkers, all of whom have been influenced slightly differently from each other. Each individual has his or her own "take" on the gospel and its spirit, a meaning significant to their own life. This collection reflects their myriad views and their subtle distinctions of expression and thought. It is through such subtleties that we can gain new perspectives and perhaps shed light on our own personal struggles in life.

In compiling the collection we have attempted to represent a variety of denominational perspectives, so not all entries will reflect everyone's shade of faith. But reading statements by individuals with whom you think you may not have much in common can often yield interesting results. Roman Catholics, for example, may discover that they have more sympathy with the thoughts of the Reformers John Calvin (1509–1564) and Martin Luther (1483–1546) than they expected. Christian groups, mainstream and the unorthodox, from various historical periods and cultural backgrounds, all have their say. St. Anthony the Abbot, the fourth-century ascetic from the Egyptian desert, rubs shoulders in this book with the Danish philosopher Søren Kierkegaard (1813–1855), and with the U.S. general Omar Bradley (1893–1981). Certain essential themes, such as peace, become the common ground for individuals, each contributing different understandings and perspectives from different situations.

For those interested in the doctrinal debates of the Christian era, key elements of some issues are touched upon in the following pages, and may inspire further reading. Early Church views on the figure of Christ or social integration among members of disparate backgrounds, or the observations of such beacons of the faith as St. Francis and St. Clare of Assisi (c. 1194–1253), provide fascinating signposts to the Church's gradual progression toward its present broad tapestry of views. And indeed, the hue and cry of the Christian faith is among its most distinguishing and engaging features. But the religious edifice as a whole yields a collective sense of spiritual value that sustains its integrity. In feeding on the morsels thrown up by the extraordinary sea of faith contained in *1,001 Pearls of Bible Wisdom* we hope you will leave the book feeling uplifted, encouraged, consoled, maybe even strengthened, and that you will return again and again, each time to be recharged and further nourished!

The Divine

In the Beginning   14

Mystic Communion   34

Heaven   52

Angels   68

The Word   85

Grace   94

IN THE BEGINNING

1   **On high** "Lift up your eyes on high and see: Who created these?"
    ISAIAH 40:26

2   **Void** "... when God created the heavens and the earth, the earth
    was a formless void and darkness covered the face of the deep.... "
    GENESIS 1:1–2

3   **From nothing** "God creates out of nothing. Therefore, until a
    man is nothing God can make nothing out of him."
    MARTIN LUTHER (1483–1546), GERMANY

4   **Accidental birth?** "That the universe was formed by a
    fortuitous concourse of atoms, I will no more believe than that
    the accidental jumbling of the alphabet would fall into a most
    ingenious treatise of philosophy."
    JONATHAN SWIFT (1667–1745), ENGLAND

5   **Poor disguise** "Nature is too thin a screen; the glory of the
    omnipresent God bursts through everywhere."
    RALPH WALDO EMERSON (1803–1882), USA

6   **SIX DAYS OF CREATION**
      While other creation accounts of the ancient
      Near East depict a cosmic struggle between the
      divine and primordial matter, the God of the
      Book of Genesis is presented as a sovereign of
      the universe who directs the work of creation
      in six days. The repeated refrain, "And there
      was evening and there was morning," have led
      some scholars to believe that the creation story
      may originally have been a hymn or poem.

---

7   **Dating the world** In the age of science, theologians
      pondered the date of creation. One 17th-century Anglican
      declared, "Heaven and earth ... were created ... in the same
      instant, on October 23, 4004BC, at nine o'clock in the morning."
      DR. JOHN LIGHTFOOT (1602–1675), ENGLAND

8   **Nature's peace** "There is no peace more wonderful than the
      peace we enjoy when faith shows us God in all created things."
      JEAN-PIERRE DE CAUSSADE (1675–1751), FRANCE

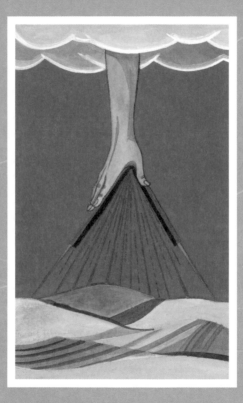

9   **Evolving art** "The world is not like a picture painted by an artist centuries ago which now hangs untouchable in a museum. It is more like a work of art in constant process of creation...."
ERNESTO CARDENAL (BORN 1925), NICARAGUA

10   **Reflection on origins** "No philosophical theory which I have yet come across is a radical improvement on the words of Genesis, that 'In the beginning God made Heaven and Earth.'"
C.S. LEWIS (1898–1963), ENGLAND

11   **Day and night** "Then God said, 'Let there be light'; and there was light. And God saw that the light was good; and God separated the light from the darkness. God called the light Day, and the darkness he called Night. And there was evening and there was morning, the first day."
GENESIS 1:3–5

12   **The gospel in nature** "God writes the gospel not in the Bible alone, but on trees, and flowers, and clouds, and stars."
MARTIN LUTHER (1483–1546), GERMANY

13   BLINDNESS AND INSIGHT
The biblical account of light entering into
the world for the first time was interpreted by
some early Christians as a symbol of Christ.
St. John the evangelist records Jesus describing
himself as "the light of the world" (John 9:5),
meaning not so much that through him people
are able to discover new things in the world,
but that, as the scholar R.H. Lightfoot (1883–
1953) suggests, he "irradiates human existence
with the knowledge of its nature, meaning
and purpose."

---

14   Shining in the dark "The people who walked in darkness
have seen a great light; those who lived in a land of deep
darkness—on them light has shined."
ISAIAH 9:2

15   Sky dome According to ancient cosmology, as well as to the
biblical authors, God had created a solid sky "dome" that held

the sun, the moon, and the stars, and that "separated the waters" below and above it (Genesis 1:7). At certain times he would open the "windows of the heavens" (Genesis 7:11) to allow rain to fall on Earth and nourish his creation.

16   **The light of knowledge** "For it is the God who said, 'Let light shine out of darkness,' who has shone in our hearts to give the light of the knowledge of the glory of God in the face of Jesus Christ."
2 CORINTHIANS 4:6

17   **Most beautiful creation** "Water is ... the most beautiful of God's creations. It is both wet and cold, heavy, and with a tendency to descend, and flows with great readiness. It is this the Holy Scripture has in view when it says, 'And the darkness was upon the face of the deep. And the Spirit of God moved upon the face of the waters.' ... [It] purifies from all filth, and not only from the filth of the body but from that of the soul, if it should have received the grace of the Spirit."
ST. JOHN OF DAMASCUS (c. 675–c. 749), SYRIA

18 Leviathan The Old Testament refers to a powerful sea monster, Leviathan, whom God created with all the other living creatures. Later Christian writers used the term as a symbol for the power of evil. The medieval theologian St. Thomas Aquinas (1225–1274) described Leviathan as the "demon of envy," while in his epic poem *Paradise Lost*, the English poet John Milton (1608–1674) compared the monster to God's adversary Satan.

19 Natural philosophy "Every flower of the field, every fiber of a plant, every particle of an insect, carries with it the impress of its Maker, and can ... read us lectures on ethics or divinity."
SIR THOMAS POPE BLOUNT (1649–1697), ENGLAND

20 Nature's book As a child, the Spanish surrealist painter Salvador Dalí (1904–1989), a devout Christian, would spend hours observing animals, plants, and stones. He referred to nature as "... the great book, always open and which we should make an effort to read." In this book, he says, God is revealed to us; "... the other books are taken from it, and in them there are the mistakes and misinterpretations of men."

21   **Lights in the sky** "'Let there be lights in the dome of the sky to
separate the day from the night; and let them be for signs and
for seasons and for days and years, and let them be lights in the
dome of the sky to give light upon the earth.' And it was so. God
made the two great lights—the greater light to rule the day and
the lesser light to rule the night—and the stars."
GENESIS 1:14–16

22   **Joyous abandon** On the last two days of creation, the Earth is
animated with creatures. The accounts in Genesis that describe
this process are filled with a sense of joyous abandon, as though
these beings represent the culmination of God's plan. At the
end of the sixth day, God reflects upon his work and notes, "It
was very good."

23   **Earth's inspiration** The Earth that abounds with "living
creatures of every kind" (Genesis 1:24) is a constant source of
inspiration to the faithful. St. Francis of Assisi (c. 1182–1226),
patron saint of animals and birds, constantly thanked God for his
"brother and sister creatures." And the English churchman

William Paley (1743–1805) declared, "It is a happy world after all. The air, the earth, the water, teem with delighted existence ... myriads of happy beings crowd upon my view."

24   **In the image of God** "Then God said, 'Let us make humankind in our image ... and let them have dominion over the fish of the sea, and over the birds of the air, and over the cattle, and over all the wild animals of the earth, and over every creeping thing.'"
GENESIS 1:26

25   **The smallest thing** "Also in this He shewed me a little thing, the quantity of an hazel-nut, in the palm of my hand; and it was as round as a ball. I looked thereupon with the eye of my understanding, and thought: What may this be? And it was answered generally thus: It is all that is made. I marveled how it might last, for methought it might suddenly have fallen to naught for little[ness]. And I was answered in my understanding: It lasteth, and ever shall [last] for that God loveth it. And so Allthing hath their Being by the love of God."
MOTHER JULIAN OF NORWICH (1342–c. 1416), ENGLAND

26   ORIGIN OF HUMANKIND

The Book of Genesis (Genesis 2:4–25) gives a clear indication of exactly how humankind came into being: God molded man from the inert "dust of the ground," in much the same way as a potter might knead clay. Life is given to him via the breath of God, which is "breathed into his nostrils" (Genesis 2:7). Adam then becomes a "living being." He is separated from the animals, given the task of naming "every living creature," and charged with ruling the Earth. To assist him in this duty, Eve, the first woman, is fashioned—thus gesturing toward the essential harmony and complementarity of the universe.

---

27   God's purpose "In the beginning God fashioned Adam, not because he had need of human beings, but so that he might have beings on whom to bestow his benefits."

ST. IRENAEUS (c. 130–c. 202), ASIA MINOR (TURKEY)

28   **Spare rib** "And the rib that the Lord God had taken from the man he made into a woman and brought her to the man. Then the man said, 'This at last is bone of my bones and flesh of my flesh; this one shall be called Woman, for out of Man this one was taken.'"
GENESIS 2:22–23

29   **Equal partner** "Eve was not made out of his head to top him, nor out of his feet to be trampled upon by him, but out of his side to be equal with him, under his arm to be protected, and near his heart to be loved."
MATTHEW HENRY (1662–1714), ENGLAND

30   **Satan's serpent** The serpent that appears in Genesis, although deceitful, was not considered by the Jews of the Old Testament period to be evil. It is not until later, in the Book of Revelation, that the snake is identified with Satan, and as God's enemy: a cosmic struggle takes place between the forces of good and evil, between "... that ancient serpent, who is called the Devil and Satan, the deceiver of the whole world" (Book of Revelation 12:9).

31   **All are one** "... there is no longer male and female; for all of you are one in Christ Jesus."
GALATIANS 3:28

32   **Abundant beauty** "The creation is quite like a spacious and splendid house, provided and filled with the most exquisite and the most abundant furnishings. Everything in it tells us of God."
JOHN CALVIN (1509–1564), FRANCE

33   **Joy of life** "As one sits ... and listens to the cuckoo and all the other bird songs, the crackling and buzzing of insects, as one gazes at the shining colors of flowers, doth one become dumbstruck before the Kingdom of the Creator."
CARL VON LINNÉ (1707–1778), SWEDEN

34   GARDEN OF EDEN

The Garden of Eden was created by God for the enjoyment of human beings (the Hebrew word *eden* means "pleasure" or "delight"). It is thought to refer to an area between the rivers Tigris and Euphrates. Mythically, the garden is a verdant paradise. Death and sickness are unknown to its inhabitants, Adam and Eve. But the continued blessedness of their existence depends upon their caring properly for the land—a duty entrusted to them by God.

---

35   Nature's steward "The Lord God took the man and put him in the garden of Eden to till it and keep it."
GENESIS 2:15

36   Life's opportunity "God set man in paradise, giving him the opportunity to advance, so that by ... becoming mature, and by sharing in the divine life, he might thus ascend to heaven. For man was created in an intermediate state, neither entirely mortal

nor wholly immortal, but capable of becoming either."
ST. THEOPHILUS OF ANTIOCH (DIED 180), SYRIA

37 **Rewards** "To everyone who conquers, I will give permission to
eat from the tree of life that is in the paradise of God."
REVELATION 2:7

38 **Love of creation** "Thus does the world forget You, its Creator,
and falls in love with what You have created instead of with You."
ST. AUGUSTINE OF HIPPO (354–430), NORTH AFRICA

39 **Gate to paradise** Followers of the Eastern Orthodox church
believe that the sword placed at the gate of Paradise, "... flaming
and turning to guard the way to the tree of life...." (Genesis
3:24), was lifted at the birth of Christ to allow humanity in.

---

40 **THE FALL**
According to Genesis, God places Adam in the
Garden of Eden and forbids him to eat from
the Tree of Knowledge. But the serpent tempts

Eve into knowing good and evil by eating fruit from the tree. She, in turn, urges Adam to taste it. As a punishment for this original sin, God expels the couple from the garden. The main interpretation of their wrongdoing is that human sin is rooted in the desire to be God-like. The urge to know all and to place oneself, instead of God, at the heart of the universe alienates humanity from God.

41　**Self-rule** "Adam switched off from God's design. Instead of maintaining his dependence on God, he took his rule over himself and thereby introduced sin into the world."
OSWALD CHAMBERS (1874–1917), SCOTLAND

42　**Adam redeemed** The ancient Hebrews regarded the Fall of humankind as an historical event that took place when Adam's disobedience in the Garden of Eden caused sin to enter the world. But St. Paul followed later Jewish thinking that Adam was not so much an historical individual as a personification of humankind (in Hebrew *adam* means "human being"). As the apocryphal 2 Baruch states, "Each of us has become our own Adam." St. Paul saw Christ as the second Adam (Romans 5 and I Corinthians 15), by whose grace we are saved. As Martin Luther (1483–1546) claimed, faith in Christ "kills the old Adam" in us.

---

43   THE FLOOD

The corruption of the world results in God's decision to bring a deluge to destroy "all flesh in which is the breath of life" (Genesis 6:17). Only Noah—"a righteous man," who "found favor in the sight of the Lord" (Genesis 6:8–9)—his family, and a male and female of every living creature were spared. After 40 days in an ark, the flood waters receded and the Earth was repopulated with Noah's descendants. Noah is therefore regarded as the second father of humankind after Adam.

---

44   God's regret "The Lord saw that the wickedness of humankind

was great in the earth, and that every inclination of the thoughts of their hearts was only evil continually. And the Lord was sorry that he had made humankind on the earth."
GENESIS 6:5–6

45 **Choices** "It was he [the Lord] who created humankind in the beginning, and he left them in the power of their own free choice."
ECCLESIASTICUS 15:14

46 **Noah's ark** Early Christians drew parallels between Noah's ark and the nascent church, which had to brave stormy times in order to survive. In Peter's first epistle, the salvation of Noah's family from the waters is said to "prefigure" (1 Peter 3:21) the salvation of souls through Christian baptism.

47 **Cleansing the world** In bringing a great flood to punish humans for their sins, it is believed that God was also "baptizing" or cleansing the earth with water. And from this act a new beginning emerged: "The water of baptism destroys one life and reveals another: it drowns the old man and raises up the new.

To be baptized is to be born according to Christ; it is to receive existence, to come into being out of nothing."

NICOLAS CABASILAS (DIED 1371), GREECE

48   THE TOWER OF BABEL

In the final pages of Genesis, humankind's urge to be God-like is represented in the building of a tower: "Let us build ourselves a city, with its top in the heavens." But God foils the presumptuous plan by confusing their language, "so that they will not understand one another's speech" (Genesis 11:7). The incomplete structure is named Babel, after the Hebrew *balal*, "to confuse." The story is thought to be a mythical explanation for the world's diversity of languages. The tower envisaged by the biblical author was a stepped temple-structure known as a ziggurat; the location is thought to be the old civilization of Babylon.

49 **God's choice?** "What really interests me is whether God had any choice in the creation of the world."
ALBERT EINSTEIN (1879–1955), GERMANY/USA

50 **The fool** "Fools say in their hearts, 'There is no God.'"
PSALM 14:1

51 **A stupendous fabric** "The wisdom and goodness of the Maker plainly appears in the parts of this stupendous fabric, and the several degrees and ranks of creatures in it."
JOHN LOCKE (1632–1704), ENGLAND

52 **One for all** "The world has been created for everyone's use..."
AMBROSE OF MILAN (339–397), ITALY

53 **Every grain of sand** "Love all of God's creation, the whole of it and every grain of sand. Love every leaf, every ray of God's light! Love the animals, love the plants, love everything. If you love everything, you will soon perceive the divine mystery in things..."
FYODOR DOSTOYEVSKY (1821–1881), RUSSIA

54   **Mystical paradox** "One of the great paradoxes of the mystical life is this: that a man cannot enter into the deepest center of himself and pass through that center into God, unless he is able to pass entirely out of himself and empty himself and give himself to other people in the purity of a selfless love."
THOMAS MERTON (1915–1968), USA/NEW ZEALAND

55   **Straight to the heart** Friedrich Schleiermacher (1768–1834) was a German philosopher, theologian, and pastor whose work had a strong impact on Christian thought. In *On Religion* (1799) he claims that religion is "… essentially an intuition and a feeling … the miracle of direct relationship with the infinite."

56   **Holy sigh** "God is an unutterable sigh in the Human Heart."
HENRY HAVELOCK ELLIS (1859–1939), ENGLAND

57   **Nothing but straw** Italian theologian St. Thomas Aquinas (1225–1274) made a huge contribution to Christian thinking. His five-volume *Summa Theologiae* covered such diverse subjects as creation, human nature, and the virtues. Aquinas placed supreme value on mystical communion—his experiences of the divine through silent contemplation proved far more instructive than his academic pursuits. He eventually gave up writing altogether and concentrated instead on meditation. He pronounced, "All that I have written seems to me nothing but straw ... compared to what I have seen and what has been revealed to me."

58 VISIONS OF THE PROPHETS

The Old Testament prophets reported many mystical experiences. Mysterious objects or scenes normally hidden from human sight were beheld and interpreted as indicators of divine purpose. These visions would seize the prophet's imagination, evoking powerful feelings. Symbolic images, like dreams with a message, were often a feature of the experience. Although the prophets had these visions in particular historical contexts, their symbolic character still holds meaning today.

59 **Intimate union** Pseudo-Dionysius the Areopagite (c. 500), a mystical theologian, believed that God and the soul share an intimate union. He claimed that knowledge of God and the gradual deification of humankind could be achieved by a process of "unknowing," by emptying the mind of all thought.

60 **Meeting God** Many mystics have tried to describe the wonderful experience of their soul uniting with God. St. Catherine of Siena (c. 1345–1380) said simply, "Then the soul is in God and God in the soul, just as the fish is in the sea and the sea in the fish."

61 **Divine harmony** "Even as music demands an interpreter before it can flood the soul with its divine harmony, so God demands an interpreter before the heart can recognize that which it forever seeks and craves to know and feel."
JOHN WILHELM ROWNTREE (1868–1905), ENGLAND

---

62 **THE EPIPHANY**
The divine nature of Christ is revealed to three wise men (Magi) who come from the East in

search of him. Their sign is a bright star which they follow from its rising to a place near Jerusalem, where it stops. They enter the house where Mary is with her newborn child and offer gifts of "gold, frankincense, and myrrh" (Luke 2). This event is known as the Epiphany and is celebrated in the Christian calendar by a festival held on January 6th (also called Twelfth Night).

---

63   Indwelling Christ "I am crucified with Christ: nevertheless I live; yet not I, but Christ liveth in me, and the life which I now live in the flesh I live by the faith of the Son of God, who loved me, and gave himself for me."
GALATIANS 2:20 [KJV]

64   Finding ourselves "To find our own centre is the reverse of becoming self-centred. It is to awaken to the centre beyond ourselves, whence we are created and to which we return with Christ, the centre where we find ourselves and Him...."
JOHN MAIN (1926–1982), ENGLAND

65 **The mystical path** St. Teresa of Avila (1515–1582) was one
of the greatest of the Spanish mystics. Her inspiring work *The
Interior Castle* (1577) identifies seven stages, represented as sets
of rooms, in the soul's spiritual quest for union with God. At first
the soul learns the importance of such virtues as humility, prayer,
and perseverance. Within the "inner rooms" of the castle, the soul
feeds on nourishment from the church in sermons, confessions,
and scripture until it is fully grown. Like a silkworm, the soul spins
its cocoon—representing Christ—in which it grows. When fully

grown, the silkworm dies, only to become a butterfly. Similarly, the soul has to die to the world before it can be united with God.

66 **A heavenly plan** St. Paul said that in Christ we can see the plan of salvation that the Father has in store for us. Mystic union is a foretaste of that heavenly state of blessedness: "With all wisdom and insight he has made known to us the mystery of his will, according to his good pleasure that he set forth in Christ, as a plan for the fullness of time" (Ephesians 1:8–9).

67 **A quiet place** Pave the way for deeper communion with God by focusing on the sounds of silence:
"Elected silence, sing to me
and beat upon my whorlèd ear,
pipe me to pastures still and be
the music that I care to hear."
GERARD MANLEY HOPKINS (1844–1889), ENGLAND

68 **Still small voice** "When we speak with God, our power of addressing him, of holding communion with him, and listening

to his still small voice, depends upon our will being one and
the same with his."

FLORENCE NIGHTINGALE (1820–1910), ENGLAND

69   THE TRANSFIGURATION OF JESUS

The mysterious episode of the Transfiguration
is a key moment in the story of Jesus' ministry.
Witnessed by Peter, James, and John, Jesus
ascends a mountain and appears to be
transformed, such that "his face shone like the
sun, and his clothes became dazzling white"
(Matthew 17:2), like those of an angel. As Peter
is speaking, "a bright cloud overshadowed
them" and a voice from within the cloud says,
"'This is my Son, the Beloved; with him I am
well pleased; listen to him!'" (Matthew 17:5).
As well as affirming the divinity of Jesus, the
story is thought to be a foreshadowing of his
resurrection, when he ascends to heaven.

70   **Power of myth** "At his Transfiguration Christ showed his disciples the splendor of his beauty, to which he will shape and color those who are his: 'He will reform our lowness configured to the body of his glory' (Philippians 3:21)."
WILLIAM BARCLAY (1907–1978), SCOTLAND

71   **Voices from Paradise**
"And I know that such a person—whether in the body or out of the body I do not know; God knows—was caught up into Paradise and heard things that are not to be told, that no mortal is permitted to repeat."
2 CORINTHIANS 12:3–4

72   **Mystery of religion**
Drawing on his experience of eastern religions, German theologian Rudolf Otto (1869–

1937) coined the word "numinous" to describe the feelings of attraction and awe that a mystic experiences in an encounter with the divine.

73 **Listen and you will hear** "If we have listening ears, God speaks to us in our own language, whatever that language is."
MAHATMA GANDHI (1869–1948), INDIA

74 **Journey to God** In the 13th century the French nun Marguerite Porete wrote *Mirror of Simple Souls*, in which she outlined seven stages in the soul's journey to God: Touched by grace, the soul follows God's commandments to **"love him with all her heart, and her neighbour also as herself" (75)**; The scorning of wealth and prestige, and **not minding material loss (76)**; **Abandoning the will to God (77)**; **Exaltation by Love through contemplation (78)**; The soul is **changed by divine light into "Love's nature" (79)**;

the soul recognizes her nothingness. In this state the soul can see divine goodness and become "wholly at rest;" **Blindness to herself or God within her (80)**, and the soul is illumined; **Glorification of the soul (81)**, though we know nothing about it until death.

82 **Like a bridal couple** In his famous work *The Spiritual Canticle*, St. John of the Cross (1542–1591) uses the theme of bridal mysticism expressed in the Bible's *Song of Songs* to interpret the love between man and God. The stages of development of the relationship between bride and bridegroom represent the stages of the mystical journey. Simple but arresting images are used throughout:
"My loved one is the mountains
The lonely wooded valleys
The strange islands
The rushing streams
The hushing of the amorous winds."

83 **Mystical wedding** A heart is the emblem of St. Catherine of

Siena (1347–1380), based on the legend that she exchanged hearts with Christ. From childhood she had visions of Jesus and would dictate her impassioned revelations. Embracing God's love, she said, was like being "clothed in a wedding garment;" but before it can be worn, you must "divest yourself of all self-love."

84 **Road less easy** The mystical path will involve pain as well as joy. To reach the "point of burning love of Christ," as the English medieval mystic Richard Rolle (1290–1349) expressed it, requires discipline and commitment. According to him, the empty values of the world should be rejected. The soul's attachment to the world has to be broken before union with the divine can be achieved. And this will mean seeking the road less easy.

85 **Return to youth** The German visionary nun and poet St. Hildegard of Bingen (1098–1179) was so famous for her insight that even popes and emperors sought her advice. When close to God, she felt "warmed" by the "living light" igniting within her chest. Even her sadness at being old would, she said, evaporate as she felt "the green shoots" of youth in her soul again.

86   **The comfort of Mary** For Catholics, the Virgin Mary is the "heart of the Church," the mother of Jesus who hears the prayers of the afflicted. The Italian monk Gabriel Possenti (1838–1862) encapsulated her role in the life of the church when he said, "If you are in danger, she will hasten to free you; if you are troubled, she will console you; if you are sick, she will bring you relief; if you are in need she will help you." No matter who you are, "she simply comes to a heart that wants to love her."

87   **Be silent** "There is hardly ever a complete silence in our soul, God is whispering to us well-nigh incessantly. Whenever the sounds of the world die out in the soul, or sink low, then we hear these whisperings of God. He is always whispering to us, only we do not always hear, because of the noise, hurry and distraction which life causes as it rushes on."
FREDERICK WILLIAM FABER (1814–1863), ENGLAND

88   **Look inside not out**
"O beauty ever ancient, ever new
Too late have I loved you.

I was outside and you were within me.

And I never found you

Until I found you within myself."

ST. AUGUSTINE OF HIPPO (354–430), NORTH AFRICA

89 **Clear the path** Among the great mystical works of the 14th century is *The Cloud of Unknowing*, written by an anonymous English monk. It claims that during the spiritual quest we will encounter a "cloud" that both prevents our understanding of the divine and enables our access to it. We must suppress all stirrings of the imagination and maintain a "blind stirring of love unto God."

---

90 **STIGMATA OF CHRIST**

One of the stranger experiences of mystic communion is the appearance of "stigmata," marks on the body resembling Christ's wounds at the Crucifixion. The concept first appears in St. Paul's letter to the Galatians: "I carry the marks of Jesus branded on my body" (Galatians 6:17). St. Francis of Assisi (c. 1181–1226) was the first known Christian to have manifested the stigmata, which he received during a retreat on a mountain. Since then more than 300 instances have been recorded.

91   Prepare your soul for God St. Francis of Sales (1567–1622) was a French mystic who was keen to enhance the spiritual growth of ordinary people. In his book *Introduction to the Devout Life*, he describes how the spiritual novice must first prepare the soul to be aware of God's presence: "Just as wherever birds fly they encounter the air, so also wherever we go or wherever we are, we find God present."

92   NATURE MYSTICISM
Many Christian mystics have had profound insights into nature. Italy's St. Francis of Assisi (c. 1182–1226) is perhaps the best known example. His famous sermon to the birds induced them "to stretch their necks, to spread their wings, to open their beaks, and to look

intently on him." The German mystic Jakob Boehme (1575–1642)—whose ideas influenced later mystics in the Romantic movement, such as William Blake and Pierre Teilhard de Chardin—talked about the essential division between the lower plain of nature and the higher spiritual plain, but said humankind must endeavor to harmonize the two. We must wait in the "deep ground" of the soul for the "sun of righteousness" to rise and increase the light of nature.

---

93 **Amid life's clamor** "In the noise and clutter of my kitchen ... I possess God in as great tranquillity as if I were upon my knees at the Blessed Sacrament."
BROTHER LAWRENCE (NICHOLAS HERMAN; c. 1605–1691), FRANCE

94 **Creation revealed** "Now I was come up in spirit through the flaming sword, into the paradise of God.... I knew nothing but pureness, and innocency, and righteousness; being renewed into the image of God by Christ Jesus, to the state of Adam, which he

was in before he fell. The creation was opened to me; and it was showed me how all things had their names given them according to their nature and virtue."
GEORGE FOX (1624–1691), ENGLAND

95   **To see infinity** The English poet William Blake (1757–1827), one of the most visionary of modern mystics, perceived divine reality and the infinite in the tiniest details of nature:
"To see a world in a grain of sand,
And a Heaven in a wild flower,
Hold Infinity in the palm of your hand,
And Eternity in an hour."

96   **Deep interfusion**
"And I have felt
A presence that disturbs me with the joy
Of elevated thoughts; a sense sublime
Of something far more deeply interfused,
Whose dwelling is the light of setting suns,
And the round ocean and the living air,

And the blue sky, and in the mind of man;
A motion and a spirit, that impels
All thinking things, all objects of all thought,
And rolls through all things...."
WILLIAM WORDSWORTH (1770–1850), ENGLAND

97 **The Jesus Prayer** In the Eastern Orthodox church it is believed that union with the divine can sometimes be achieved by meditation and frequent recitation of the Jesus Prayer: "Lord Jesus Christ have mercy on me as a sinner." The repetition produces a state of spiritual tranquillity in the practitioner and can result in the experience of holy wisdom or even a vision of the Divine Light.

HEAVEN

98   **A tent** "It is he [the Lord] who sits above the circle of the earth, and its inhabitants are like grasshoppers; who stretches out the heavens like a curtain, and spreads them like a tent to live in."
ISAIAH 40:22

99   **Wedding canopy**
"In the heavens he has set a tent for the sun, which comes out like a bridegroom from his wedding canopy, and like a strong man runs its course with joy.
Its rising is from the end of the heavens, and its circuit to the end of them; and nothing is hid from its heat."
PSALM 19:4–6

100   **Far country**
"My soul, there is a country
Far beyond the stars,
Where stands a winged sentry
All skilfull in the wars:
There, above noise and danger,
Sweet Peace sits crown'd with smiles

And One born in a manger
Commands the beauteous files."
HENRY VAUGHAN (1622–1695), WALES

101 ULTIMATE ABODE

The Bible conceives of heaven as an abode existing above the sky, the dwelling place of God and the angels, and ultimately of all the redeemed. The Christian hope and belief is that at the end of time all the faithful will eventually reside with Christ in heaven. Catholic theology asserts, for example, that the souls of the saints are waiting in heaven to be reunited with their bodies at the resurrection of the dead.

102 Community in heaven

An important part of the belief in heaven is the idea of a community in which happiness will be shared with saints, angels, and those known and loved on Earth: "Those four innocent souls that had made their way to Heaven before me, surely they would be sorry for their sister, sorely

tried on earth. They could prove that love doesn't end in death. Before long a delicious sense of peace flooded into my soul and I realized that there were people who loved me in Heaven too."
ST. TERESA OF LISIEUX (1873–1897), FRANCE

103 **Many dwelling places** "In my Father's house there are many dwelling places. If it were not so, would I have told you that I go to prepare a place for you? And if I go and prepare a place for you, I will come again and will take you to myself, so that where I am, there you may be also."
JOHN 14:2–3

104 **Here and now** "It is certain that all that will go to heaven hereafter begin their heaven now, and have their hearts there."
MATTHEW HENRY (1662–1714), ENGLAND

105 **Backdrop to existence** "Heaven is not a space overhead to which we lift our eyes; it is the background of our existence, the all-encompassing lordship of God within which we stand."
HELMUT THIELICKE (1908–1966), GERMANY

106 **In awe** "Two things fill me with constantly increasing admiration and awe, the longer and more earnestly I reflect on them: the starry heavens without and the moral law within."
IMMANUEL KANT (1724–1804), GERMANY

107 **A safe place** "... store up for yourselves treasures in heaven, where neither moth nor rust consumes and where thieves do not break in and steal."
MATTHEW 6:20

108 **In my soul** "I have found my heaven on earth, because heaven is God, and God is in my soul."
ELIZABETH OF THE TRINITY (1880–1906), FRANCE

109 **PARABLES OF THE KINGDOM OF HEAVEN**
Many of Jesus' parables concern the kingdom of heaven. These short, metaphorical stories, or aphorisms, use everyday contexts to convey spiritual meaning. Their very nature requires them to be interpreted, and their meaning is

not always clear. For Jesus, the kingdom seems sometimes to point to a future apocalyptic event, sometimes to a mysterious reality.

110   **The secrets of beyond** "Then the disciples came and asked him, 'Why do you speak to them in parables?' He answered, 'To you it has been given to know the secrets of the kingdom of heaven, but to them it has not been given.'"
MATTHEW 13:10–11

111   **The sower** "The kingdom of heaven may be compared to someone who sowed good seed in his field; but while everybody was asleep, an enemy came and sowed weeds among the wheat, and then went away. So when the plants came up and bore grain, then the weeds appeared as well. And the slaves of the householder came and said to him, 'Master, did you not sow good seed in your field? Where, then, did these weeds come from?' He answered, 'An enemy has done this.' The slaves said to him, 'Then do you want us to go and gather them?' But he replied, 'No; for in gathering the weeds you would uproot the

wheat along with them. Let both of them grow together until the harvest.... [Then] collect the weeds first and bind them in bundles to be burned, but gather the wheat into my barn.'"

MATTHEW 13:24–30

112   **Mustard seed** "The kingdom of heaven is like a mustard seed that someone took and sowed in his field; it is the smallest of all the seeds, but when it has grown it is the greatest of shrubs and becomes a tree, so that the birds of the air come and make nests in its branches."

MATTHEW 13:31–32

113   **Equal in eternity** "In heaven, to be even the least is a great thing, where all will be great; for all shall be called the children of God."

THOMAS À KEMPIS (c. 1380–1471), GERMANY

114   **Humble yourself** "... the disciples came to Jesus and asked, 'Who is the greatest in the kingdom of heaven?' He called a child, whom he put among them, and said, "Truly I tell you,

unless you change and become like children, you will never enter the kingdom of heaven.'"
MATTHEW 18:1–3

115 **My heaven** The French nun St. Teresa of Lisieux (1873–1897) died at the tender age of 24 from tuberculosis. But on her deathbed she vowed not to remain idle in heaven: "... my mission is soon to begin—to make others love God as I love him ... to teach souls my little way. I will spend my heaven doing good on earth. This is not impossible, for the angels in heaven watch over us. No, there can be no rest for me till the end of the world...."

116 **The next step** "Heaven is not to be looked upon only as the reward, but as a natural effect, of a religious life."
JOSEPH ADDISON (1672–1719), ENGLAND

117 **Desire** "The access to Heaven is through desire. He who longs to be there really is there in spirit. The path to Heaven is measured by desire and not by miles."
ANONYMOUS (*THE CLOUD OF UNKNOWING*, 14TH CENTURY), ENGLAND

118 **The finest pearl** "Again, the kingdom of heaven is like a merchant in search of fine pearls; on finding one pearl of great value, he went and sold all that he had and bought it."
MATTHEW 13:45–46

119 **Unspoken voice**
"The heavens are telling the glory of God; and the firmament proclaims his handiwork.
Day to day pours forth speech, and night to night declares knowledge.

There is no speech, nor are there words; their voice is not heard; yet their voice goes out through all the earth, and their words to the end of the world."

PSALM 19:1–4

---

120   THE ASCENSION OF CHRIST
Ascension Day is a major feast of the Christian year and marks the return of Christ, in human form, to heaven. Of the four evangelists, only St. Luke records this event: while Jesus was blessing the disciples at Bethany, "he withdrew from them and was carried up into heaven." In Acts 1:1–3, Luke states that this took place 40 days after the Resurrection; Jesus spent the intervening period instructing his apostles and "speaking about the kingdom of God."

---

121   Know yourself "And the Kingdom of heaven is within you and whosoever knoweth himself shall find it."

OXYRHYNCHUS SAYINGS OF JESUS, EGYPT

122   **Pure joy** "Joy is the serious business of heaven."
C.S. LEWIS (1898–1963), ENGLAND

123   **With open arms** St. Catherine of Genoa (1447–1510) was a
wealthy Genoese citizen before she converted to Christianity to
help the destitute. Catherine had visions about the nature of
heaven and the soul: "I see Paradise has no gate, but whosoever
will may enter therein, for God is all mercy and stands with open
arms to admit us to His glory. But still I see that the Being of God
is so pure ... that should a soul see in itself even the least note of
imperfection, it would rather cast itself into a thousand hells than
go with that spot into the presence of the Divine Majesty."

124   **Celestial bliss** The 16th-century Italian Jesuit Robert Bellarmine
pointed out that the Bible teaches us that on entering heaven not
that the joy of the Lord will enter us, but that we will enter the
joy of the Lord. This, he believes, is "... proof that the joy will be
greater than we can conceive. We shall enter into a great sea of
divine and eternal joy, which will fill us within and without, and
surround us on all sides."

125   **Ever-flowing wisdom** "How great, how lovely, how certain is the knowledge of all things there [in heaven], with no error and no trouble, where the wisdom of God shall be imbibed at its very source with no difficulty and with utmost happiness!"
ST. AUGUSTINE OF HIPPO (354–430), NORTH AFRICA

126   **Resurrection** "When we rise again with glorious bodies ... these ... will be white and resplendent as the snow, more brilliant than the sun, more transparent than crystal, and each one will have a special mark of honour and glory, according to the support and endurance of ... sufferings ... freely borne to the honour of God."
JAN VAN RUYSBROECK (1293–1381), BELGIUM

127   **Surely unworthy?** "I confess that I am bewildered and lose myself at the thought of the divine goodness, a sea without shore and fathomless, of God who calls me to an eternal rest after such short time of labour, here summons and calls me to Heaven, to that supreme Good that I sought so negligently, and promises me the fruit of those tears that I shed so sparingly."
ALOYSIUS GONZAGA (1568–1591), ITALY

128   **What lies beyond?** Grief-stricken after his wife's death, the English scholar and essayist on Christian morals C.S. Lewis (1898–1963) reflected on heaven and immortality. He concluded, "Heaven will solve our problems, but not, I think, by showing us subtle reconciliations between all our apparently contradictory notions. The notions will all be knocked from under our feet. We shall see that there never was any problem."

129   **DAY OF JUDGMENT**
According to Christian theology, at some point there will be a general resurrection of the dead when humanity as a whole will be judged. Also known as the Last Judgment, this idea of a final reckoning was prevalent at the time of Jesus' life. Jews looked forward to release from earthly oppression and to a future existence in heaven. But there were, and still are, various interpretations of this "end time."

130   **Meaning of heaven** "'Resurrection' means a life that bursts
through the dimensions of space and time in God's invisible,
imperishable, incomprehensible domain. This is what is meant by
'heaven'—not the heaven of the astronauts, but God's heaven. It
means going into reality, not going out."
HANS KUNG (BORN 1928), SWITZERLAND

131   **God's love** "Understand what heaven is: It is but the turning in
of the will into the Love of God. Wheresoever thou findest God
manifesting himself in love, there thou findest heaven, without
travelling for it so much as one foot."
JAKOB BOEHME (1575–1624), GERMANY

132   **The wedding banquet** In Matthew's gospel (Matthew
22:1–14) Jesus compares the kingdom of heaven to a wedding
banquet. According to the narrative, the king is dismayed that
no guests attend his son's wedding. In an attempt to solve the
problem, he invites complete strangers, society's outcasts, and
this time the wedding hall was "filled with guests." The lesson
to be learned is that the call to join Christ in heaven goes out to

many, yet those who accept the offer are not always the people
we might expect.

133   Have no fear
"No coward soul is mine,
No trembler in the world's storm-troubled sphere:
I see Heaven's glories shine,
And faith shines equal, arming me from fear."
EMILY BRONTË (1818–1848), ENGLAND

134   An apocalyptic vision "And the armies of heaven, wearing
fine linen, white and pure, were following him on white
horses."
REVELATION 19:14

135   No darkness nor dazzling
"Bring us, O Lord God, at our last awakening,
into the house and gate of heaven,
to enter that gate and dwell in that house,
where there shall be no darkness nor dazzling,

but one equal light;
no noise nor silence, but one equal music;
no fears nor hopes, but one equal possession;
no ends nor beginnings, but one equal eternity;
in the habitations of thy glory and dominion,
world without end."
JOHN DONNE (1572–1631), ENGLAND

136   One minute

"Take all the pleasures of all the spheres,
And multiply each through endless years—
One minute of heaven is worth them all."
THOMAS MOORE (1779–1852), IRELAND

137   Mists and vapors

"We see but dimly through the mists and vapors;
Amid these earthly damps
What seem to us but sad, funereal tapers
May be heaven's distant lamps."
HENRY LONGFELLOW (1807–1882), USA

ANGELS

138   **Unseen spirits**
"Millions of spiritual Creatures walk the Earth
Unseen, both when we wake and when we sleep."
JOHN MILTON (1608–1674), ENGLAND

139   **In your presence** "Make yourself familiar with the angels
and behold them frequently in spirit; for without being seen,
they are present with you."
ST. FRANCIS OF SALES (1567–1622), FRANCE

---

140   **DIVINE MESSENGERS**
Angels appear frequently in the Old and New
Testaments. Essentially spirit-beings, they act
as God's messengers, ensuring communication
between heaven and Earth, God and humans
(the English word "angel" is derived from the
Greek *angelos*, meaning "messenger"). The
Bible describes the angels traveling up and
down a ladder that stretches from heaven to
Earth (Genesis 28:11–12), busy performing the

many tasks entrusted to them by God—from warning, punishment, and admonition to protection, annunciation, and reassurance.

141 **Warning of disaster** "When morning dawned, the angels urged Lot, saying 'Get up, take your wife and your two daughters who are here, or else you will be consumed in the punishment of the city.'" GENESIS 19:15 16

142 **In praise of God** "Bless the Lord, O you his angels, you mighty ones who do his bidding, obedient to his spoken word."
PSALM 103:20

143 **Three wise men** "The Lord appeared to Abraham by the oaks of Mamre, as he sat at the entrance of his tent in the heat of the day. He looked up and saw three men standing near him. When he saw them, he ... bowed down to the ground."
GENESIS 18:1–2

144 **Instruments of judgment** "So it will be at the end of the age. The angels will come out and separate the evil from the righteous and throw them into the furnace of fire, where there will be weeping and gnashing of teeth."
MATTHEW 13:49–50

---

145 **SPIRIT HIERARCHY**
The 6th-century mystical theologian Pseudo-Dionysius the Areopagite developed a system of classifying spirit-entities that was accepted

by the church as the standard categorization. In his *Celestial Hierarchy*, Dionysius identified three hierarchies of angels, each consisting of three choirs arranged in the following order. Top triad: seraphim, cherubim, and thrones; middle triad: dominations, virtues, and powers; lower triad: principalities, archangels, and angels. Of these nine orders only the last two were believed to have direct contact with humankind.

---

146 · **The throne of God** Seraphs are charged with looking after the throne of God. The prophet Isaiah describes a member of the angelic order of seraphs as having "... six wings: with two they covered their faces, and with two they covered their feet, and with two they flew" (Isaiah 6:2). Their incessant gyrating movement generates intense heat—St. Francis of Assisi (c. 1181–1226) claimed to have had a vision of their fiery form—which, together with their chant of "Holy, holy, holy is the Lord of hosts" (Isaiah 6:3), keeps away "the shadows of darkness," according to Pseudo-Dionysius the Areopagite (6th century).

147   **Jacob's ladder** In the Old Testament, Jacob is reassured of God's presence in a dream transmitted by angels. "Taking one of the stones of the place, he put it under his head and lay down in that place. And he dreamed that there was a ladder set up on the earth, the top of it reaching to heaven; and the angels of God were ascending and descending on it."
GENESIS 28:11–12

148   **Heavenly vigil** Each of the seven spheres of heaven is assigned to one of the seven archangels: Gabriel, Raphael, Michael, Uriel, Jophiel, Zadkiel, and Samael (Satan). Gabriel and Michael are the two most important archangels in the Christian tradition. Gabriel features in the Book of Daniel, and foretells the births of John the Baptist and of Jesus Christ. Michael is the helper of the Chosen People, and St. John the Divine says he fights the dragon in his apocalypse. In the early church, Michael was believed to aid Christian armies in battle against the infidel and to protect individual Christians against evil. In the Book of Tobit, Raphael is described as one of seven holy angels who present the prayers of the saints to the "Holy One."

149 THE ANGEL OF THE LORD
The angel of the Lord is distinct from other angels. Whenever a momentous event is about to take place in the Old Testament, this being appears as a direct representative of God—often to prepare humans for divine intervention.

---

150 **An idea of God** Mystics may be able to come close to God when their souls reach their greatest spiritual heights, but as one of the foremost German visionaries, Meister Eckhart (c. 1260–c. 1328), proclaimed, "An angel gives a closer idea of Him. That is all an angel is: an idea of God."

151 **Special helper** The Italian Catholic priest St. John of Bosco (1815–1888) founded a religious order known as the Salesian Society (named after the mystic St. Francis of Sales) to help the poor and orphaned boys of Turin. His teaching was based on love and encouragement rather than on punishment. In his attempt to redirect the lives of the boys he would advise them, "When tempted, invoke your [guardian] angel. He is more eager to help than you are to be helped! Ignore the devil and do not be afraid of him: he trembles and flees at your guardian angel's sight."

152 **Burning bush** "[Moses] led his flock beyond the wilderness, and came to Horeb, the mountain of God. There the angel of the Lord appeared to him in a flame of fire out of a bush; he looked, and the bush was blazing, yet it was not consumed."
EXODUS 3:1–2

153 **The Other World**
"Sweet souls around us watch us still,
Press nearer to our side;
Into our thoughts, into our prayers,
With gentle helpings glide."
HARRIET BEECHER STOWE (1811–1896), ENGLAND

154 **Meadows and forget-me-nots**
"Silently, one by one, in the infinite meadows of heaven,
Blossomed the lovely stars, the forget-me-nots of the angels."
HENRY WADSWORTH LONGFELLOW (1802–1882), USA

155 GUARDIAN ANGELS

Some Christians believe that everyone has been given a guardian angel. The Church Fathers taught that at birth we receive a guardian angel whose role it is to carefully protect and guide us through life and direct our souls to salvation. They do not have the ability to influence human will directly, but they are able to conjure up images in the imagination. Guardian angels can work on the human senses by outwardly assuming a visible form, or inwardly, by what we term today as intuition. We can communicate our thoughts and wishes to angels only through prayer.

---

156 Sparing the Israelites "... when he sees the blood on the lintel and on the two doorposts, the Lord will pass over that door and will not allow the destroyer [the angel of destruction] to enter your houses to strike you down."
EXODUS 12:23

157 **Angelic inspiration** "An angel can illumine the thought and mind of man by strengthening the power of vision, and by bringing within his reach some truth which the angel himself contemplates."
ST. THOMAS AQUINAS (1225–1274), ITALY

158 **On watch** "For he will command his angels concerning you to guard you in all your ways. On their hands they will bear you up, so that you will not dash your foot against a stone."

PSALM 91:11–12

159   **Angels of the churches** In the Revelation of St. John the Divine, messages are sent to the angels of the seven churches of Asia Minor. Classically the number seven is identified with the number of heavens, and the apocalypse is intended to fire the imagination of its readers to believe in a future time when present tribulation will be overcome. The seven angels are protectors of their churches.

---

160   **LUCIFER AND THE REBEL ANGELS**
When Lucifer was cast out of heaven by God, his band of rebel angels fell with him. By New Testament times, a celestial war was believed to have taken place in which good angels were allied with God against Lucifer (identified with Satan) and his demonic angels. One early Church Father, Theodore of Mopsuetia,

interpreted these fallen angels as being actual men, rather than demons, who submitted to Lucifer and became his instruments, spreading sin through the world.

---

161   **Flash of lightning** "He [Jesus] said to them, 'I watched Satan fall from heaven like a flash of lightning. See, I have given you [the seventy missionaries] authority to tread on snakes and scorpions, and over all the power of the enemy; and nothing will hurt you."
LUKE 10:18–19

162   **In their own language** "The angels are so enamored of the language that is spoken in heaven that they will not distort their lips with the hissing and unmusical dialects of men, but speak their own, whether there be any who understand it or not."
RALPH WALDO EMERSON (1803–1882), USA

163   **Power corrupts** "The desire for power caused the angels to fall; the desire for knowledge in excess caused man to fall, but in charity there is no excess, neither can angel nor man come in danger."

FRANCIS BACON (1561–1626), ENGLAND

164 **Hovering angel** "O welcome, pure-eyed Faith, white-handed Hope, thou hovering angel, girt with golden wings."

JOHN MILTON (1608–1674), ENGLAND

---

165 **THE ANNUNCIATION**

The Annunciation—the announcement to Mary by the archangel Gabriel of the forthcoming birth of Jesus—is one of the key moments in the Christian story. The miraculous conception of the Son of God in the womb of the Virgin Mary is commemorated by the Church with a feast day. Since medieval times this has been accompanied by the recitation of the prayer "Ave Maria," based on the passage in Luke's gospel that describes the event.

166   **Samson, deliverer of Israel** "And the angel of the Lord appeared to the woman and said to her, 'Although you are barren, having borne no children, you shall conceive and bear a son. Now be careful not to drink wine or strong drink, or to eat anything unclean, for you shall conceive and bear a son. No razor is to come on his head, for the boy shall be a nazirite [one consecrated] to God from birth. It is he who shall begin to deliver Israel from the hand of the Philistines."
JUDGES 13:3–5

167   **Birth of John the Baptist** "I am Gabriel. I stand in the presence of God, and I have been sent to speak to you and to bring you this good news."
LUKE 1:19

168   **Visitation to Mary** "In the sixth month the angel Gabriel was sent by God to a town in Galilee called Nazareth, to a virgin engaged to a man whose name was Joseph, of the house of David. The virgin's name was Mary."
LUKE 1:26–27

169   **A son foretold** "The angel said to her, 'Do not be afraid, Mary,
for you have found favor with God. And now, you will conceive
in your womb and bear a son, and you will name him Jesus. He
will be great, and will be called the Son of the Most High, and
the Lord God will give to him the throne of his ancestor David.
He will reign over the house of Jacob forever, and of his kingdom
there will be no end.'"
LUKE 1:30–33

170   **Shepherds' watch** "In that region there were shepherds living
in the fields, keeping watch over their flock by night. Then an
angel of the Lord stood before them, and the glory of the Lord
shone around them."
LUKE 2:8–9

171   **Holy messengers** "You should know that the word 'angel'
denotes a function rather than a nature. Those holy spirits of
heaven have always been spirits, but they can only be called
angels when they deliver a message."
POPE ST. GREGORY I, THE GREAT (c. 540–604), ITALY

172 **Revealing the mysteries** "They [angels] take different forms at the bidding of their master, God, and thus reveal themselves to men and unveil the divine mysteries to them."
ST. JOHN OF DAMASCUS (c. 675– c. 749), SYRIA

173 **Spirit offspring** "An angel is a spiritual being created by God without a body, for the service of Christendom and the Church."
MARTIN LUTHER (1483–1546), GERMANY

174 **The Second Coming** "For the Son of Man is to come with his angels in the glory of his Father, and then he will repay everyone for what has been done."
MATTHEW 16:27

THE WORD

175 **With God** "In the beginning was the Word, and the Word was with God, and the Word was God."
JOHN 1:1

176 **Creation through Him** In his letter to the Christians at Colossae in Asia Minor, the apostle Paul refers to a hymn about the eternal nature of Christ. The creative power of God, associated with Wisdom in the Old Testament, is now linked with Christ, which John the evangelist identifies with the Word that existed before creation: "For in him all things in heaven and on earth were created, things visible and invisible.... He himself is before all things, and in him all things hold together" (Colossians 1:16–17).

177 **Proper sustenance**
"... one does not
live by bread alone,
but by every word
that comes from the
mouth of the Lord."
DEUTERONOMY 8:3

178 **To have purpose** "For as the rain and the snow come down from heaven and do not return there until they have watered the earth, making it bring forth and sprout ... so shall my word be that goes out from my mouth; it shall not return to me empty, but it shall accomplish that which I purpose."
ISAIAH 55:10–11

179 **Creatures** "Every creature is a divine word because it proclaims God."
BONAVENTURE (1221–1274), ITALY

180 **A discerning sword** "Indeed, the word of God is living and active, sharper than any two-edged sword, piercing until it divides soul from spirit, joints from marrow; it is able to judge the thoughts and intentions of the heart."
HEBREWS 4:12

181 **Mocked** "For the word of the Lord has become for me a reproach and derision all day long."
JEREMIAH 20:8

182   **Night rescuer** "For while gentle silence enveloped all things, and night in its swift course was now half gone, your all-powerful word leaped from heaven, from the royal throne, into the midst of the land that was doomed."
WISDOM OF SOLOMON 18:14–15

---

183   **WORD OF THE PROPHETS**
In the Bible the revelation of God takes the form, primarily, of the spoken word. The phrase "the word of God" therefore assumes a major role in the biblical tradition. The prophets of the Old Testament became the mouthpiece of God, through whom people might know his will. Thus Jeremiah begins his prophecy, "the word of the Lord came to me" (Jeremiah 1:11).

---

184   **Holy word** "The only pure and all-sufficient source of the doctrines of faith is the revealed word of God, contained now in the holy Scriptures."
ST. PHILARET OF MOSCOW (1782–1867), RUSSIA

185 **Power of the word** "The meek and mild mediocrity of most of us stands in sharp contrast to that volcanic, upheaving, shaggy power of the prophets [the spokesmen of God], whose descendants we were meant to be."
THOMAS KELLY (1893–1941), USA

186 **Divine utterance** "... no prophecy of scripture is a matter of one's own interpretation, because no prophecy ever came by human will, but men and women moved by the Holy Spirit spoke from God."
2 PETER 1:20–21

187 **About me** "When you read God's word, you must constantly be saying to yourself, 'It is talking to me, and about me.'"
SØREN KIERKEGAARD (1813–1855), DENMARK

188 **Spiritual nourishment** St. Mary of Egypt (c. 344–421) renounced a life of prostitution and became a hermit. She is said to have lived alone for almost 50 years, nourished by wild herbs and God's word: "When I think of from what evils the Lord had freed me, I am nourished by incorruptible food.... I feed upon and cover myself with the Word of God, who contains all things."

189   THE INCARNATION

Greek philosophers in New Testament times combined their concept of wisdom, or *logos* (literally meaning "word" or "reason"), with biblical accounts of the "word" of God, as spoken through the Old Testament prophets. The idea of an eternal entity, the Word, was conveyed by John the evangelist who identified it specifically with Christ: "And the Word became flesh and lived among us" (John 1:14). For the first time the Word became an historical manifestation of God on Earth in bodily form.

190   **Face of God** "The Word is the face, the countenance, the representation of God, in whom he is brought to light and made known."

ST. CLEMENT OF ALEXANDRIA (c. 150–c. 215), GREECE/EGYPT

191 **To become divine** The main authority of the early church on the Incarnation, or the Word made Flesh, was the Egyptian theologian St. Athanasius (c. 296–373). He maintained that by adopting human form the Word restored the image of God to fallen man, thereby effecting a spiritual healing of humanity: "By the Word becoming man ... the very Word of God has been made known. For he became human that we might become divine; he revealed himself in a body that we might understand the unseen Father."

192 **Word as reason** The 2nd-century theologian St. Justin Martyr argued that Christianity was the most rational of all philosophies. He taught that the Word of God became human in order to reveal the truth, that humankind shares in divine "reason," or *logos*. Only Christians live

"reasonably with the Word," since it is only in Christ that the full *logos* is found.

193 **Spiritual birth** "Out of love for us the Word of God, born once for all in the flesh, wills continually to be born in a spiritual way in those who desire him."
ST. MAXIMUS THE CONFESSOR (c. 580–662), GREECE

194 **Divine conundrum?** "He was created of a mother whom he created. He was carried by hands that he formed. He cried in a manger in wordless infancy, he the Word, without whom all human eloquence is mute."
ST. AUGUSTINE OF HIPPO (354–430), NORTH AFRICA

195 **Soul food** "The words of God which you receive by your ear, hold fast in your heart. For the Word of God is the food of the soul."
POPE ST. GREGORY I, THE GREAT (c. 540–604), ITALY

196 **Fascination** "The Word of God is not a sounding but a piercing word, not pronounceable by the tongue but efficacious in the

mind, not sensible to the ear but fascinating to the affection."
ST. BERNARD OF CLAIRVAUX (1090–1153), FRANCE

197 THE WORD IN THE CHURCH

In the New Testament, Luke describes how the apostles receive the Holy Spirit at Pentecost and immediately afterwards begin preaching. The event is a dramatic one, with the place in which they are praying being "shaken" by the presence of the Holy Spirit. Thereafter they "spoke the word of God with boldness" (Acts 4:31). The word, or authority, of God is thought to have then passed from the apostles to the Church Fathers.

198 **Seeds of salvation** "The pre-existent Word, the preserver of all things, gives the seeds of true wisdom and salvation to his disciples. He enlightens them and gives them understanding in the knowledge of his Father's kingdom."
EUSEBIUS OF CAESAREA (c. 260–c. 340), PALESTINE

199   **Of the wise** "Let the word of Christ dwell in you richly; teach and admonish one another in all wisdom...."
COLOSSIANS 3:16

200   **Despite faults** "Wherever we see the Word of God purely preached and heard, there a church of God exists, even if it swarms with many faults."
JOHN CALVIN (1509–1564), FRANCE

201   **Transcendental hearing** "It is precisely in transcending even the highest reach of the human mind, in passing beyond all symbols and expressions of itself, that faith reveals itself in its essential purity. This is the essential 'void' in which alone the human is open to and able to hear the eternal Word."
DIETRICH BONHOEFFER (1906–1945), GERMANY

202   **Take heed** Be attentive to God's word, "... as to a lamp shining in a dark place, until day dawns and the morning star rises in your hearts."
2 PETER 1:19

GRACE

203 **As allotted** "... each of us was given grace according to the measure of Christ's gift."
EPHESIANS 4:7

204 **Necessity of grace** "Nothing whatever pertaining to godliness and real holiness can be accomplished without grace."
ST. AUGUSTINE OF HIPPO (354–430), NORTH AFRICA

205 **In nature** "Grace does not abolish nature but perfects it."
ST. THOMAS AQUINAS (1225–1274), ITALY

206 **Like a perfume** "He who aspires to the grace of God must be pure, with a heart as innocent as a child's. Purity of heart is to God like a perfume sweet and agreeable."
ST. NICHOLAS OF FLÜE (1417–1487), SWITZERLAND

207 **Humbling of the Son**
"Thou Son of the Blessed, what grace was
manifest in thy condescension!
Grace brought thee down from heaven;

Grace stripped thee of thy glory;
Grace made thee poor and despicable;
Grace made thee bear such burdens of sin,
Such burdens of sorrow, such burdens of
God's curse as are unspeakable."
JOHN BUNYAN (1628–1688), ENGLAND

208 **To the humble** "Grace is always given to those ready to give thanks for it, and therefore it is wont to be given to the humble man, and to be taken from the proud man."
THOMAS À KEMPIS (c. 1380–1471), GERMANY

---

209 **DOCTRINE OF GRACE**
Christians believe that humankind, as a result of the Fall, is inclined by nature to sin, and is therefore incapable of achieving salvation without the help of God. Some argue that we are so sinful that to do any good deed requires divine grace. As St. Paul says, the recipients of God's grace perform deeds of grace. This

grace is so powerful that it can move men and women to work miracles. In the Old Testament, those who found "favor" with God—Noah, for example—performed "gracious" deeds. But it is through Christ that humankind has the unique opportunity to find salvation in God's grace, to be redeemed by him (Romans 3:24 & 5:2&9).

---

210 **Heavenly city** "Citizens are born into the earthly city by a nature spoiled by sin, but they are born into the heavenly city by grace freeing nature from sin."
ST. AUGUSTINE OF HIPPO (354–430), NORTH AFRICA

211 **Protective grace** The Psalmist in the Old Testament sometimes beseeches God: "Be gracious to me, O Lord, for I am languishing; O Lord heal me, for my bones are shaking with terror" (6:2). Likewise in 41:4, "O Lord be gracious to me; heal me, for I have sinned against you." Elsewhere in the Old Testament, God's protection of his people is evident as grace, even though the term is often not used. So in Deuteronomy (32:10), it is recorded that

God "sustained" Jacob "in a howling wilderness waste; he shielded him, cared for him, guarded him as the apple of his eye."

212   **From infancy** Divine grace comes to rest on Jesus from infancy, when "the favor of God was upon him" (Luke 2:40). As he grew, all who encountered him were amazed at his "gracious words," meaning that they seemed to come from God. And like a man given divine protection, Jesus passes through their midst unharmed when a mob tried to hurl him off the edge of a cliff (Luke 4:22–30).

---

213   **THE GRACE AT PENTECOST**
According to the New Testament, after Christ ascended to heaven the apostles were left alone on Earth to continue preaching the gospel. One day the Holy Spirit descended on them, gracing them with the power to do this work effectively. Henceforth the apostles and all those who followed the faith were imbued with a new life in the Spirit. The event is recorded in

Acts of the Apostles and tells of "a sound like the rush of a violent wind" that filled the house where they were assembled, and a "tongue, as of fire" that rested on each apostle. "All of them were filled with the Holy Spirit" (Acts 2:2–4). God's grace is evident here in his direct intervention to reinvigorate and strengthen his followers. Christians celebrate this significant day as Pentecost.

---

214   **After tribulation** "Our Lord and Saviour lifted up his voice and said with incomparable majesty: 'Let all men know that grace comes after tribulation. Let them know that without the burden of afflictions it is impossible to reach the height of grace. Let them know that the gifts of grace increase as the struggles increase.'" ST. ROSE OF LIMA (1586–1617), PERU

215   **Sweet salvation** A famous hymn written by an Anglican priest who was once a seafaring slave-trader expresses the true wonder of God's grace:

"Amazing grace, how sweet the sound
That sav'd a wretch like me!
I once was lost, but now am found,
Was blind, but now I see."
JOHN NEWTON (1725–1807), ENGLAND

216   **Spiritual gifts** Paul the apostle recognized that individuals are graced with particular talents, which he called "gifts of healing by the one Spirit." Some individuals are wise, others knowledgeable, or perceptive; some have great faith, others the ability to heal. Whatever the gift, these manifestations of the Holy Spirit are not to be a source of personal pride, since they are "for the common good" (1 Corinthians 12:7–10).

217   **Human restoration** "Man is born broken. He lives by mending. The grace of God is glue."
EUGENE O'NEILL (1888–1953), USA

218   **Give with grace** "How should Our Lord fail to grant his graces to him who asks for them from his heart when He confers so

many blessings even on those who do not call on Him? Ah, He would not so urge and almost force us to pray to Him if He had not a most eager desire to bestow His graces on us."
ST. JOHN CHRYSOSTOM (c. 347–407), ASIA MINOR (TURKEY)

219 **Infinite variety** "Why did Christ refer to the grace of the Spirit under the name of water? Because through water all vegetables and animals live. Because the water of rain comes down from heaven, and though rain comes down in one form its effects take many forms. Yea, one spring watered all of paradise, and the same rain falls on the whole world, yet it becomes white in the lily, red in the rose, purple in the violet."
ST. CYRIL OF JERUSALEM (c. 310–386), PALESTINE

220 **SPEAKING IN TONGUES**
Some Christians consider speaking in tongues, or *glossolalia*, to be among the gifts conferred via the grace of the Holy Spirit. The phenomenon was said to be a common feature of the early church; today it exists within

Pentecostal churches and some branches of mainstream Christian denominations, where it is known as Charismatic Renewal. Adherents believe in the possibility of receiving the same gifts from the Spirit as the early Christians. Although the words uttered form no part of a recognized language and are incomprehensible, it is believed that they can be interpreted or translated by those with a special gift.

---

221   **Where the wind blows** John the evangelist likened the Spirit, the purveyor of God's grace, to the wind. "The wind blows where it chooses, and you hear the sound of it, but you do not know where it comes from or where it goes" (John 3:8).

222   **Melted into holy love** "O Holy Ghost, that givest grace where Thou wilt, come into me and ravish me to Thyself. The nature that Thou didst make, change with honeysweet gifts, that my soul, filled with Thy delightful joy, may despise and cast away all the things of this world, that it may receive ghostly gifts, given

by Thee, and going with joyful songs into infinite light may be all melted in holy love."

RICHARD ROLLE (c. 1295–1349), ENGLAND

223 **Anxious God** "God is more anxious to bestow His blessings on us than we are to receive them."

ST. AUGUSTINE OF HIPPO (354–430), NORTH AFRICA

224 **Do we impede God?** "There is no one who during this mortal life can properly judge how far he is an obstacle, and to what extent he resists, the workings of God's grace in his soul."

ST. IGNATIUS OF LOYOLA (c. 1491–1556), SPAIN

225 **Be careful** Paul the apostle warned his churches to guard against the abuse of grace: "As we work together with him, we urge you also not to accept the grace of God in vain" (2 Corinthians 6:1).

226 **Goodness and favor** "Grace is the free, undeserved goodness and favour of God to mankind."

MATTHEW HENRY (1662–1714), ENGLAND

227 THE EUCHARIST

One of the most sacred Christian sacraments, the Eucharist is an outward and visible sign of an inward and spiritual grace given to us by God. During the Last Supper Jesus gave his disciples bread and wine, which he identified as his body and blood: "Those who eat my flesh and drink my blood have eternal life" (John 6:54). Roman Catholics believe that an act of divine grace occurs during the performance of mass, whereby the bread and wine are mysteriously "transubstantiated," or transmuted, into the "real presence" of Christ's body and blood in the recipient. Sixteenth-century reformers, such as Ulrich Zwingli and John Calvin, claimed that the rite was symbolic but that those receiving the Eucharist also receive the power or virtue of Christ.

---

228 God's immensity "In proportion to the size of the vessel of

Virtues

The Commandments 108

Love & Kindness 118

Wisdom & Truth 129

Forgiveness & Reconciliation 138

Repentance & Confession 146

Patience & Endurance 157

Humility 163

Courage & Fortitude 172

Duty 183

Prudence 190

THE COMMANDMENTS

232   **Bringer of wisdom** "If you desire wisdom, keep the commandments, and the Lord will lavish her upon you."
ECCLESIASTICUS 2:26

233   **No slavish obedience** "If a commandment is kept through fear of punishment and not for love of righteousness, it is kept slavishly, not freely, and therefore is not truly kept at all. For fruit is good only if it grows from the root of love."
ST. AUGUSTINE OF HIPPO (354–430), NORTH AFRICA

234   MOSES ON MOUNT SINAI
The book of Exodus tells how Moses ascends Mount Sinai to receive the divine laws from God—the most important of these are known as The Ten Commandments or Decalogue. Thereafter Moses was identified as the "lawgiver." As the only person permitted to speak directly to God, his role was unique.

---

235   The Commandments The Ten Commandments (Exodus 20:1–17) are Christianity's code of ethics. They represent the covenant between God and his people and define their duties to him, to one another, and to society: **"You shall have no other gods before me" (236)** requires devotion to God alone; **"You shall not make for yourself an idol" (237)** forbids the worship of human or animal objects (Exodus 32 shows how the Israelites violate this code when they build a golden calf, which they worship as a god); **"You shall not make wrongful use of the name of the Lord your God" (238)** disallows inappropriate use of God's name; **"Remember the sabbath day, and keep it holy"**

(239) enjoins people to rest on the seventh day. The following four commandments are self-explanatory: **"Honor your father and your mother" (240)**; **"You shall not murder" (241)**; **"You shall not commit adultery" (242)**; **"You shall not steal" (243)**. **"You shall not bear false witness against your neighbor" (244)** prohibits lying; **"You shall not covet your neighbor's house; you shall not covet your neighbor's wife, or male or female slave, or ox, or donkey, or anything that belongs to your neighbor" (245)** forbids envy.

246 **Temporary tutor** "... the law was our disciplinarian until Christ came, so that we might be justified by faith."
GALATIANS 3:24

247 **Light on sin** "... through the law comes the knowledge of sin."
ROMANS 3:20

248 **Too severe?** "Most people really believe that the Christian commandments (for example, to love one's neighbor as oneself) are intentionally a little too severe—like putting the clock ahead

half an hour to make sure of not being late in the morning."
SØREN KIERKEGAARD (1813–1855), DENMARK

249   **A rule for life** "When you are disturbed, do not sin; ponder it
on your beds, and be silent."
PSALM 4:4

250   **A misunderstanding** "If envy was not such a tearing thing to
feel it would be the most comic of sins. It is usually ... based on
a complete misunderstanding of another person's situation."
MONICA FURLONG (1930–2003), ENGLAND

251   **How to survive** "The Ten Commandments, completed by
the evangelical precepts of justice and charity, constitute the
framework of individual and collective survival."
POPE JOHN XXIII (1958–1963), ITALY

252   **Bringer of life** According to the book of Leviticus, the value of
the Law, as contained in the commandments, is life-enhancing,
since by keeping God's statutes, "one shall live" (Leviticus 18:5).

253 **Seed in the soul** "The Ten Commandments ... had their existence in man and lay as a seed hidden in ... his soul."
WILLIAM LAW (1686–1761), ENGLAND

254 **FAITH AND THE LAW**
The Law was given to Moses by God so that people might live righteously. However, Paul said Christians were "justified [made righteous] by faith in Christ" because "no one will be justified by the works of the law" (Galatians 2:16). By this he did not mean that the Law should no longer be obeyed but that the Jews were now joined by the Gentiles (non-Jews), as a "wild olive shoot [is] ... grafted ... to share the rich root of the olive tree." (Romans 11:17).

255 **Banish your worldly desires** "Holy obedience puts to shame all natural and selfish desires. It mortifies our lower nature and makes it obey the spirit and our fellow men."
ST. FRANCIS OF ASSISI (c. 1182–1226), ITALY

256 **Keep on track** "Do not weary of reading the commandments of the Lord, and you will be adequately instructed by them so as to know what to avoid and what to go after."
ST. BERNARD OF CLAIRVAUX (1090–1153), FRANCE

257 **Enlighten us** "God, enlighten the darkness of my heart and give me a right faith, a sure hope, a perfect charity, sense and knowledge, so that I may carry out your holy ... command."
ST. FRANCIS OF ASSISI (c. 1182–1226), ITALY

258 **No theft?** Many scholars believe that the commandment, "You shall not steal," was an injunction against kidnapping people and subjecting them to a life of slavery or servitude.

259 **Longing to hear** "The unfolding of your words gives light; it imparts understanding to the simple. With open mouth I pant,

because I long for your commandments."
PSALM 119:130–131

260 **With all your heart** "You shall love the Lord your God with all your heart, and with all your soul, and with all your might."
DEUTERONOMY 6:5

261 **No greater love** "This is my commandment, that you love one another as I [Jesus] have loved you. No one has greater love than this, to lay down one's life for one's friends."
JOHN 15:12–13

262 **On entering the Promised Land** "... keep all his [God's] ... commandments ... so that your days may be long."
DEUTERONOMY 6:1–2

263 **Have confidence in God** "What God commands, that is good."
LUDWIG WITTGENSTEIN (1889–1951), AUSTRIA

264 **The greatest commandment** "Teacher, which commandment in the law is the greatest? He said to him, 'You shall love the Lord your God with all your heart, and with all your soul, and with all your mind.' This is the greatest and first commandment. And a second is like it: **'You shall love your neighbor as yourself' (265)**. On these two commandments hang all the law and the prophets."

MATTHEW 22:36–40

266 **In need of grace** "Reawaken my soul by the grace of your love, since it is your commandment that we love you with all our heart and strength, and no one can fulfill that commandment without your help."

JOHN OF ALVERNIA (1259–1322), ITALY

267 **Repeated breaking of the law** "We have broken God's commandments again and again, and in the court of God's presence we are manifestly guilty. I believe it is only because Jesus actually took our sin and God's righteous judgment upon Himself that we are saved."

DAVID WATSON (1933–1984), ENGLAND

268   **Hope for the future** The prophet Ezekiel looked forward to God's blueprint for a stable future: "I will put my spirit within you, and make you follow my statutes and be careful to observe my ordinances" (Ezekiel 36:27).

269   **Sterile without devotion** "A state of temperance, sobriety and justice without devotion is a cold, lifeless, insipid condition of virtue, and is rather to be styled philosophy than religion."
JOSEPH ADDISON (1672–1719), ENGLAND

270   **In good faith** "If you begin to grieve at this, to judge your superior, to murmur in your heart, even though you outwardly fulfill what is commanded, this is not the virtue of obedience, but a cloak over your malice."
ST. BERNARD OF CLAIRVAUX (1090–1153), FRANCE

271   **Virtue of obedience** "Obedience is the perfection of the religious life; by it man submits to man for the love of God, as God rendered Himself obedient unto men for their salvation."
ST. THOMAS AQUINAS (1225–1274), ITALY

[117]

LOVE & KINDNESS

272 **Unity** "Love is life. All, everything that I understand, I understand because I love. Everything is united by it alone. Love is God, and to die means that I, a particle of love, shall return to the general and eternal source."
LEO TOLSTOY (1828–1910), RUSSIA

273 **Without beginning and end**
"Love Was without beginning, Is and Shall Be without ending."
MOTHER JULIAN OF NORWICH (1342–c. 1416), ENGLAND

274 **The apple of his eye** God's tender love of his people is expressed in Deuteronomy, when he cares for Moses, whom he "sustained in a desert land." God "shielded him, cared for him, guarded him as the apple of his eye" (32:10).

275 **Committed love** "If you heed these ordinances ... the Lord your God will maintain with you the covenant loyalty that he swore to your ancestors; he will love you, bless you, and multiply you."
DEUTERONOMY 7:12–13

276   **Steadfast love** The prophet Hosea (Hosea 11) uses imagery of love and parenthood to describe the relationship between God and his chosen people. God desires "steadfast love" from his people, not the empty gesture of routine sacrifices.

277   **Unconditional love** "... God proves his love for us in that while we still were sinners Christ died for us."
ROMANS 5:8

---

278   **THE CROSS**
A key message of Christianity is that humankind is redeemed through the love of God. As John says, "God so loved the world that he gave his only Son" (John 3:16) who died on the Cross. This is the ultimate sacrifice, committed in an act of love. The verse continues, "so everyone who believes in him may not perish but may have eternal life." Eternal life will be granted to those who take the essential leap of faith.

279 **Inseparable bond** "For I am convinced that neither death, nor life, nor angels, nor rulers, nor things present, nor things to come ... nor anything else in all creation, will be able to separate us from the love of God in Christ Jesus our Lord."
ROMANS: 8:38–39

280 **Divine gift** According to St. Paul, "God's love has been poured into our hearts through the Holy Spirit" (Romans 5:5). Love originates from God, not the human heart. It is a divine gift.

281 **Two selves** "I saw in myself two sides and it was as if these had been separated by a furrow. On one side I saw fullness of love and every good, which was from God and not from me. On the other side I saw myself as arid and saw that nothing good originated in me .... I discovered that it was not I who loved ... but that which loved in me came from God alone."
ANGELA OF FOLIGNO (1248–1309), ITALY

282 **Love is** "Love is patient; love is kind; love is not envious or boastful or arrogant or rude. It does not insist on its way; it is

not irritable or resentful; it does not rejoice in wrongdoing, but rejoices in truth. It bears all things, believes all things, hopes all things, endures all things."
1 CORINTHIANS 13:4–7

283   **A cymbal** "If I speak in the tongues of mortals and of angels, but do not have love, I am a noisy gong or a clanging cymbal."
1 CORINTHIANS 13:1

284   **All that matters** "... the only thing that counts is faith working through love."
GALATIANS 5:6

285   **Greatest virtue** "And now faith, hope, and love abide, these three; and the greatest of these is love."
1 CORINTHIANS 13:13

286 **City of God** "Two cities have been formed by two loves: the earthly city by the love of self, leading to the contempt of God, and the heavenly city by the love of God, leading to contempt of self. The former glories in itself, the latter in the Lord."
ST. AUGUSTINE OF HIPPO (354–430), NORTH AFRICA

287 **A mother's love** The prophet Isaiah uses the analogy of a mother's love for her child to portray the depth of God's love for his people: "Can a woman forget her nursing child, or show no compassion for the child of her womb?" (Isaiah 49:15)

288 **Love's progression** "Now that you have purified your souls by your obedience to the truth so that you have genuine mutual love, love one another deeply from the heart."
1 PETER 1:22

289 **God is love** "Whoever does not love does not know God, for God is love."
1 JOHN 4:7–8

290 **Love's law** "... you shall love your neighbor as yourself."
LEVITICUS 19:18

291 **Moses' request** "Owe no one anything except to love one another; for the one who loves another has fulfilled the law."
ROMANS 13:8

292 **Blind love** Peter says if we love one another, we will not see each other's faults, as "love covers a multitude of sins" (1 Peter 4:8).

293 THE CHRISTIAN COMMUNITY
John the evangelist emphasizes the ethical dimension of love within the community. Drawing on a speech by Jesus, he says: "A new command I [Jesus] give you: Love one another" (John 13:34–35). Mutual love would be the hallmark of the disciples' devotion to Christ.

---

294 All-embracing love "Love all God's creation ... every grain of sand in it. Love every leaf, every ray of God's light.... If you love everything, you will perceive the divine mystery in things. Once you have perceived it ... you will ... love the world with an all-embracing love."
FYODOR DOSTOYEVSKY (1821–1881), RUSSIA

295 No limits "Love feels no burden, thinks nothing of trouble, attempts what is above its strength, pleads no excuse of impossibility; for it thinks all things lawful for itself, and all things possible."
THOMAS À KEMPIS (c. 1380–1471), GERMANY

296   **Stairway to heaven** "Christ made love the stairway that would enable all Christians to climb up to heaven. So hold fast to love in all sincerity, give each other practical proof of it, and by your progress in it, make your ascent together."
ST. FULGENTIUS OF RUSPE (468–533), NORTH AFRICA

297   **Find compassion** "Rejoice with those who rejoice, weep with those who weep."
ROMANS 12:15

298   **God's kindness** "As for me, I am poor and needy, but the Lord takes thought for me."
PSALM 40:17

299   **A poor woman's offering**
Mark tells the story of Jesus in the temple watching people put their gifts into the offering box.

Many of the rich gave large amounts of money, but then a poor widow came along and put in just two small coins. Jesus tells his disciples that despite her modest offering, she contributed more than all the other people combined—they had given only what they did not need, whereas her love and kindness were so great that "... out of her poverty [she] has put in everything she had, all she had to live on" (Mark 12:44).

300 **Essence of Christianity** "The whole being of any Christian is Faith and Love.... Faith brings the man to God, love brings him to men."
MARTIN LUTHER (1483–1546), GERMANY

301 **Into God** "The more a man loves, the more deeply does he penetrate into God."
ST. CLEMENT OF ALEXANDRIA (c. 150–c. 215), GREECE/EGYPT

302 **Cast out all fear** "There is no fear in love, but perfect love casts out fear."
1 JOHN 4:18

303 **Embody God's kindness** "Be the living expression of God's kindness: kindness in your face, kindness in your eyes, kindness in your smile, kindness in your warm greeting."
MOTHER TERESA (1910–1997), INDIA

304 **Love yourself** "He who knows himself, knows everyone. He who can love himself, loves everyone."
ST. ANTHONY (c. 251–c. 356), EGYPT

305 **Labor with love** "The whole of life is but a single day, to those who labor with love."
ST. GREGORY OF NAZIANZUS (c. 330–c. 390), ASIA MINOR (TURKEY)

306 **Indestructible love** "Many waters cannot quench love, neither can floods drown it."
SONG OF SOLOMON 8:7

307 **Act of faith** "Love is an act of faith, and whoever is of little faith is also of little love."
ERICH FROMM (1900–1980), GERMANY

308   **Small task** "What does the Lord require of you but to do justice, and to love kindness, and to walk humbly with your God?"
MICAH 6:8

309   **Pure love** "An instant of pure love is more precious to God and the soul, and more profitable to the church, than all other good works together, though it may seem as if nothing were done."
ST. JOHN OF THE CROSS (1542–1591), SPAIN

310   **Learn to love** "Life is learning to love and most of us have merely begun when we die. This is the main reason why many of us long for and expect another life."
DAME CICELY SAUNDERS (1918–2005), ENGLAND

311   **Give, and feel more** "It is better to love than be loved."
ST. FRANCIS OF ASSISI (c. 1182–1226), ITALY

312   **Beauty of the soul** "Since love grows within you, so beauty grows. For love is the beauty of the soul."
ST. AUGUSTINE OF HIPPO (354–430), NORTH AFRICA

WISDOM & TRUTH

313 **So noble** "Truth is something so noble that if God could turn aside from it, I could keep to the truth and let God go."
MEISTER ECKHART (c. 1260–c. 1328), GERMANY

314 **A wise silence** "Even fools who keep silent are considered wise; when they close their lips, they are deemed intelligent."
PROVERBS 17:28

315 **Divine wisdom** "For the Lord gives wisdom; from his mouth come knowledge and understanding; he stores up sound wisdom for the upright."
PROVERBS 2:6

316 **An uncomfortable truth**
"'What is truth?' said jesting Pilate, and would not stay for an answer."
FRANCIS BACON (1561–1626), ENGLAND

317 **Three wise men** "... after Jesus was born ... wise men from the East came to Jerusalem, asking, 'Where is the child who has been born king of the Jews? For we observed his star at its rising, and have come to pay him homage.'"
MATTHEW 2:1–2

318 **Knowledge versus wisdom** "Knowledge is proud that he has learned so much; Wisdom is humble that he knows no more."
WILLIAM COWPER (1731–1800), ENGLAND

319 **God's folly** Paul identifies Jesus with the "wisdom of God" (1 Corinthians 1:24) because wisdom originates from the beginning of time: "the Lord created me [wisdom] at the beginning of his work" (Proverbs 8:22). He contrasts worldly wisdom with the folly of the cross, for "God's foolishness is wiser than human wisdom" (1 Corinthians 1:25).

320 **Neither greatness nor age** "It is not the old that are wise, nor the aged that understand what is right."
JOB 32:9

321 **Seek and you will find** "The beginning of wisdom is found in doubting; by doubting we come to the question, and by seeking we may come upon the truth."
PETER ABELARD (1079–1142), FRANCE

322 **Two kinds of wisdom** In the epistle of James, the author talks of two kinds of wisdom. One is earthly, born of "ambition," and is "boastful and false to the truth" (3:14). The other kind comes from above and is "pure, then peaceable, gentle, willing to yield" (3:17), and will produce only good will.

---

323 **SOLOMON'S WISDOM**
King Solomon was said to have been awarded his exceptional wisdom by God after he had requested "...an understanding mind to govern your people, able to discern between good and evil...." (1 Kings 3:9). Solomon is the patron of "wisdom literature" in the Bible, which combines praise of God with practical teachings. His acts of wisdom include a case of

two women claiming to be the mother of a newborn. When Solomon threatens to slice the child in two and give each woman half, the true mother said she would rather give up her claim than see the child harmed. Anticipating this reaction, the king was able to return the child to its rightful parent (1 Kings 3:16–27).

---

324 **Wisdom's call** "Does not wisdom call, and does not understanding raise her voice?"
PROVERBS 8:1

325 **Divine truth** "When the Spirit of truth comes, he will guide you into all the truth ..."
JOHN 16:13

326 **My truth** "The thing is to understand myself, to see what God really wishes me to do.... what good would it do me to be able to explain the

meaning of Christianity if it had no deeper significance for me and for my life—what good would it do me if truth stood before me, cold and naked, not caring whether I recognized her or not, and producing in me a shudder of fear rather than a trusting devotion?

SØREN KIERKEGAARD (1813–1855), DENMARK

327   **Suffer fools gladly** The people of Corinth thought themselves wise, even though they accepted teaching that was false. Paul claimed they "suffer fools gladly" (2 Corinthians 11:19) [KJV].

328   **Reflection in creatures** "Every creature is by its nature a kind of effigy and likeness of the eternal Wisdom."
BONAVENTURE (1221–1274), ITALY

329   **Tree of life** In Proverbs 3:18, Wisdom is described as "... a tree of life to those who lay hold of her."

330   **Grow wiser** "Never be ashamed to own you have been in the wrong, 'tis but saying you are wiser today than you were yesterday."
JONATHAN SWIFT (1667–1745), IRELAND

331   **Real liberty** "... the truth will set you free."
JOHN 8:32

332   **In sum** "The entire sum of our wisdom, of that which deserves to be called true and certain wisdom, may be said to consist of two parts ... the knowledge of God and of ourselves."
JOHN CALVIN (1509–1564), FRANCE

333   **Turn from evil** "Do not be wise in your own eyes; fear the Lord, and turn away from evil."
PROVERBS 3:7

335 **Wisdom's beginning** "Fear of the Lord is the beginning of knowledge; fools despise wisdom and instruction" (Proverbs 1:7)—the wise person thus follows God's commandments.

336 **The benefit of understanding** "Happy are those who find wisdom, and those who get understanding...."
PROVERBS 3:13

337 **House of knowledge** "By wisdom a house is built, and through understanding it is established...."
PROVERBS 24:3–4

338 **Fool's anger** "A fool gives full vent to his anger, but a wise man keeps himself under control."
PROVERBS 29:11

340   **The pain of knowing** "For with much wisdom comes much sorrow; the more knowledge, the more grief."
ECCLESIASTES 1:18

341   **Wise serpent** "I send you forth as sheep in the midst of wolves: be ye therefore wise as serpents, and harmless as doves."
MATTHEW 10:16 [KJV]

342   **Inseparable** "Truth and Love are wings that cannot be separated, for Truth cannot fly without Love, nor can Love soar aloft without Truth; their yoke is one of amity."
ST. EPHRAEM THE SYRIAN (c. 306–373), ASIA MINOR (TURKEY)

343   **To speak or not to speak** "... wisdom consists in knowing when and how to speak and when and where to keep silent."
JEAN PIERRE CAMUS (1582–1652), FRANCE

344   **The source of truth** "All that is true, by whomsoever it has been said, has its origin in the Spirit."
ST. THOMAS AQUINAS (1225–1274), ITALY

FORGIVENESS & RECONCILIATION

345   THE RAINBOW AND THE COVENANT
After the Flood that destroyed all living things,
except those taken into Noah's ark, God made
a covenant, or pledge, with humanity never
to devastate the Earth again. As a reminder of
his promise he placed a rainbow in the sky: "I
have set my bow in the clouds, and it shall be
a sign of the covenant...." (Genesis 9:13). The
covenant was fulfilled in the Passion of Christ.
Jesus straddles the divide between human
wrongdoing and God's judgment and, through
the Crucifixion, enables God to be reconciled
with sinful humanity. People no longer need to
endure God's wrath—their sins are forgiven.

---

346   Purpose of Christ "... in Christ God was reconciling the world to
himself, not counting their trespasses against them...."
2 CORINTHIANS 5:19

347   Saved by his life "But God proves his love for us in that while

we still were sinners Christ died for us. Much more surely then, now that we have been justified by his blood, will we be saved through him from the wrath of God...."
ROMANS 5:8–9

348 Reverence in forgiveness
"If you, O Lord, should mark iniquities,
Lord, who could stand?
But there is forgiveness with you,
so that you may be revered."
PSALM 130:3–4

349 Remission of sins "Forgiveness is the remission of sins. For it is by this that what has been lost, and was found, is saved from being lost again."
ST. AUGUSTINE OF HIPPO (354–430), NORTH AFRICA

350 Jesus and the sinful woman Luke tells the story of a Pharisee named Simon who invited Jesus to his house. A woman known to be a sinner arrived, bathed Jesus' feet in her tears, dried them with her hair, kissed them, and anointed them in ointment. The Pharisee was dismayed that Jesus allowed himself to be touched by the woman. But Jesus compared her kind actions with those of Simon, who had done nothing to welcome Jesus into his house. Jesus then forgave the woman, saying that because her sins were many, "... she has shown great love. But the one to whom little is forgiven, loves little" (Luke 7:36–48).

351 Harmonizing humanity The logical extension of reconciliation between God and humankind is the bringing together of disparate groups of people. In the epistle to the Ephesians (2:13–14), Paul says that Christ is "our peace." The Gentiles have joined with Jews. Christ has "broken down the dividing wall."

352 From humility Jesus says, "Do not judge, and you will not be judged; do not condemn, and you will not be condemned. Forgive, and you will be forgiven" (Luke 6:37).

353 The unforgiving servant Jesus told a parable of a servant whose debts were written off by his king (Matthew 18:21–35).

However, the same servant became enraged when a poor man who owed him just a small sum could not repay him, and he had him thrown into prison. The king was furious, saying, "Should you not have had mercy, as I had mercy on you?" He made the servant pay the cancelled debt. Just as we are forgiven for our wrongs, so we should forgive others for theirs.

354 Little me
"Forgive, O Lord, my little jokes on Thee
And I'll forgive Thy great big one on me."
ROBERT LEE FROST (1874–1963), USA

355 Forgive us our sins "And forgive us our sins, for we ourselves forgive everyone indebted to us."
LUKE 11:4

356 Their trespasses "For if you forgive others their trespasses, your heavenly Father will also forgive you; but if you do not forgive others, neither will your Father forgive your trespasses."
MATTHEW 6:14–15

357 Everlasting forgiveness "God pardons like a mother, who kisses the offense into everlasting forgiveness."
HENRY WARD BEECHER (1813–1887), USA

358 Make your peace "If another member of the church sins against you, go and point out the fault when the two of you are alone. If the member listens to you, you have regained that one."
MATTHEW 18:15

359 Breaking hatred "Forgiveness is the key that unlocks the door of resentment and the handcuffs of hate."
CORRIE TEN BOOM (1892–1983), HOLLAND

360 On the cross "Then Jesus said, 'Father, forgive them; for they do not know what they are doing.'"
LUKE 23:34

361 In sickness and in health Mark (2:1–12) tells the story of a paralyzed man who is lowered through the roof of a house by his friends in order to reach Jesus, who is teaching. Jesus forgives the man's sins when he sees the great faith of those who helped him. Jesus cures him physically and also cleanses him of sin.

362   **How many times?** "Then Peter came and said to him, 'Lord, if another member of the church sins against me, how often should I forgive? As many as seven times? Jesus said to him, 'Not seven times, but, I tell you, seventy-seven times.'"
MATTHEW 18:21–22

363   **Before apology** "The only true forgiveness is that which is offered and extended even before the offender has apologized and sought it."
SØREN KIERKEGAARD (1813–1855), DENMARK

364   **Conquer** "The glory of Christianity is to conquer by forgiveness."
WILLIAM BLAKE (1757–1827), ENGLAND

365   **Fuel for the fire** "Without wood a fire goes out; without gossip a quarrel dies down."
PROVERBS 26:20

REPENTANCE & CONFESSION

366 **Acknowledge guilt** In ancient Israel, guilt was regarded as a collective problem—everyone was at fault, rather than just one individual. During times of national disaster, people would gather and confess their sinfulness. Their repentance would take the form of fasting and singing songs of lamentation, in a prescribed liturgy. Many prophets called for Israel's repentance: "Return, faithless Israel," says Jeremiah, "only acknowledge your guilt" (Jeremiah 3:12–13).

367 **Inspiring a change of heart** The prophet Ezekiel looks forward to a time when God will inspire a change of heart in his people and cause them to repent of their ways. He will "sprinkle clean water" upon their heads in a symbolic act of cleansing their souls (36:25).

368 **Taking a different route** "Often we shall have to change the direction of our thinking and our wishing and our striving. That is what repentance really means—taking our bearings afresh and trying a new road."
HARRY WILLIAMS (1919–2006), ENGLAND

369   **Be honest with yourself** "Before God can deliver us we must undeceive ourselves."

ST. AUGUSTINE OF HIPPO (354–430), NORTH AFRICA

370   **JOHN THE BAPTIST**
The message of John the Baptist was that people should repent in anticipation of the Messiah's coming. The expectation was that he would not tolerate sinners and that those who did not repent would remain deaf to the message of Christ, who will "baptize with the Holy Spirit" (Matthew 3:11). John demanded a change of heart in his people if they wanted to find spiritual salvation.

371   **Listen and repent** In the Bible, the key to repentance is contained in the parables, which the disciples did not understand. Jesus, quoting from the prophet Isaiah, said, "You will indeed listen, but never understand, and you will indeed look, but never perceive. For this people's heart has grown dull, and their ears are hard of hearing, and they have shut their eyes; so that they might not look with their eyes, and listen with their ears, and understand with their heart and turn—and I would heal them" (Matthew 13:14–15).

372 **Parable of the lost sheep** "Which one of you, having a hundred sheep and losing one of them, does not leave the ninety-nine in the wilderness and go after the one that is lost until he finds it? When he has found it, he lays it on his shoulders and rejoices. And when he comes home, he calls together his friends and neighbors, saying to them, 'Rejoice with me, for I have found my sheep that was lost.' Just

so, I tell you, there will be more joy in heaven over one sinner
who repents than over ninety-nine righteous persons who need
no repentance."

LUKE 15:4–7

373   **In need of help** "When the scribes of the Pharisees saw that he
was eating with sinners and tax collectors, they said to his [Jesus']
disciples, 'Why does he eat with tax collectors and sinners?' When
Jesus heard this, he said to them, 'Those who are well have no
need of a physician, but those who are sick [do]; I have come to
call not the righteous but sinners [to repentance].'"

MARK 2:16–17

374   **Absolving sin** "You take the sinfulness from sinners, O Christ,
and when we repent you make us welcome beside you."

RABBULA OF EDESSA (DIED 436), ASIA MINOR (TURKEY)

375   **Integral to faith** "There is no faith without repentance, and
there is no church without repentance."

MARTIN NIEMOLLER (1892–1984), GERMANY

[149]

376 PETER'S DENIAL OF CHRIST

When a plot to betray Jesus was made known, the disciple Peter told him he was prepared to go with him "to prison and to death" (Luke 22:33). But after the arrest, Peter's courage failed him. Later, in the courtyard of the high priest's house, Peter was recognized by three different people, and he feared that he would be linked to Jesus. With each charge, he denied any association. But on the third denial, a cock crowed. Jesus, who must have been within sight or earshot, "turned and looked at Peter" (Luke 22:61). Peter remembered Jesus' prophecy that he would deny Christ three times before the cock crowed. In great distress, Peter "went out and wept bitterly" (Matthew 26:75). Despite his remorse, his repentance saved him—he no longer lived a lie but went on to become the "rock" of the Christian church.

377 **Just say it** "If we say that we have no sin, we deceive ourselves, and the truth is not in us. If we confess our sins, he who is faithful and just will forgive us our sins and cleanse us from all unrighteousness."
1 JOHN 1:8–9

378 **Brother in arms** "Our brother has been given to us to help us. He hears the confession of our sins in Christ's stead and he forgives our sins in Christ's name."
DIETRICH BONHOEFFER
(1905–1945), GERMANY

379 **Show it in deed** "To do so no more is the truest repentance."
MARTIN LUTHER (1483–1546),
GERMANY

380 **Wide range** "Repentance ranges from regretting obvious sins like murder … to the realization that

not loving [your brother as yourself] is a murder. 'Whoever hates his brother is a murderer' (1 John 3:15), and that an evil look is adultery and the love of praise is stealing God's glory."
ST. JOHN CHRYSOSTOM (c. 347–407), ASIA MINOR (TURKEY)

381   **Through God's eyes** "One of the most fundamental marks of true repentance is a disposition to see our sins as God sees them."
CHARLES SIMEON (1759–1836), ENGLAND

382   **Teach me how**
"Teach me how to repent for that's as good
As if thou hadst seal'd my pardon, with thy blood."
JOHN DONNE (1573–1631), ENGLAND

383   **Hold up your hand** "Often nothing requires more courage than admission of fault. The disturbance that repentance evokes in our personal and collective psyches is so jarring that we tend to exhaust every other available dynamic before we succumb. We dread the bald admission of our wrong-doing!"
SISTER JOAN PULS (BORN 1934), USA

384 **Our ultimate freedom** "The final contribution of religious faith to freedom is the freedom to confess our sins; the freedom to admit that we sit under the ultimate judgment of God."
URSULA NIEBUHR (1908–1997), ENGLAND

385 **Like an infant** "We emerge from repentance like a baby coming out of a bath."
HENRI BOULARD (20th CENTURY), EGYPT

386 **First confess** "The confession of evil works is the first beginning of good works."
ST. AUGUSTINE OF HIPPO (354–430), NORTH AFRICA

387 **Most divine** "Of all acts of man, repentance is the most divine."
THOMAS CARLYLE (1795–1881), SCOTLAND

388 **Refresh yourself** "Repent ye therefore, and be converted, that your sins may be blotted out, when the times of refreshing shall come from the presence of the Lord."
ACTS 3:19 [KJV]

389   **The palace of Christ** "A good conscience is the palace of Christ; the temple of the Holy Ghost; the paradise of delight; the standing Sabbath of the saints."

ST. AUGUSTINE OF HIPPO (354–430), NORTH AFRICA

390   **Help one another** "Therefore confess your sins to one another, and pray for one another, so that you may be healed."

JAMES 5:16

391 **Never too late** "He comes never late who comes repentant."
JUAN DE HOROZCO (DIED 1608), SPAIN

392 **Only what we are** "We must lay before Him what is in us, not what ought to be in us."
C.S. LEWIS (1898–1963), ENGLAND

393 **Pardon is always possible** "God hath promised pardon to him that repenteth, but he hath not promised repentance to him that sinneth."
ST. ANSELM (1033–1109), ENGLAND

394 **Cease sinfulness** "True repentance is to cease from sin."
ST. AMBROSE (340–397), ITALY

395 **Kneeling before God** "A man's very highest moment is, I have no doubt at all, when he kneels in the dust, and beats his breast, and tells all the sins of his life."
OSCAR WILDE (1854–1900), IRELAND

PATIENCE & ENDURANCE

396   **When the sun doesn't shine** "Though God takes the sun out of heaven, yet we must have patience."
GEORGE HERBERT (1593–1633), ENGLAND

397   **An ally** "Patience is the companion of wisdom."
ST. AUGUSTINE OF HIPPO (354–430), NORTH AFRICA

398   **Be still** "Be still before the Lord, and wait
    patiently for him;
do not fret over those who
    prosper in their way,
over those who carry out evil devices."
PSALM 37:7

399   **Precious crop** "Be patient ... until the coming of the Lord. The farmer waits for the precious crop from the earth, being patient with it until it receives the early and the late rains. You also must be patient."
JAMES 5:7–8

400 **Nature's pace** "Adopt the pace of nature; her secret is patience."
RALPH WALDO EMERSON (1803–1882), USA

401 **All things come** "We must wait for God, long, meekly, in the wind and wet, in the thunder and lightning, in the cold and the dark. Wait, and he will come."
FREDERICK FABER (1814–1863), ENGLAND

402 **Like a donkey** "How does a donkey behave? If it is slandered, it keeps silent; if it is not fed, it keeps silent ... it never complains, however much it is ... ill-used.... That is how the servant of God must behave. I stand before you, Lord, like a donkey."
PETER CLAVER (1580–1654), SPAIN

403 **ENDURANCE IN ADVERSITY**
When understood as the means by which people can endure trials sent by God, patience can be a meaningful experience and a source of joy. For the saints, it was seen as a way of strengthening their love of God in their bid for perfection. Paul encouraged his followers, saying that whatever the hardships may be, "the love of Christ urges us on" (2 Corinthians 5:14). Remaining steadfast when the way forward is fraught with danger is a deeply Christian virtue—as Jesus said, "By your endurance you will gain your souls" (Luke 21:19).

404 Movers "Patience and diligence, like faith, remove mountains."
WILLIAM PENN (1644–1718), ENGLAND/USA

405 In bloom "Obedience is the fruit of faith; patience, the bloom on the fruit."
CHRISTINA ROSSETTI (1830–1894), ENGLAND

406 Waiting has its rewards "The Lord is good to those who wait for him, to the soul that seeks him."
LAMENTATIONS 3:25

407 Turn the other cheek "Do not resist an evil-doer. But if anyone strikes you on the right cheek, turn the other also..."
MATTHEW 5:39

408 Extra mile "If anyone forces you to go one mile, go also the second mile."
MATTHEW 5:41

409 Bearing tribulation "He did submit himself unto the elements,

unto cold and heat, hunger and thirst, and other insensible creatures, concealing His power ... in order that He might teach us ... with what patience we ought to bear tribulation."
ANGELA OF FOLIGNO (1248–1309), ITALY

410   **Endurance wins** "Patient endurance attains all things."
ST. TERESA OF AVILA (1515–1582), SPAIN

411   **THE PATIENCE OF JOB**
In the Old Testament, Job is described as "blameless and upright," a man of strong character, who "turned away from evil" (Job 1:1). He is nevertheless tested by God via the agency of Satan: he loses his wealth, his health, and his ten children. But despite his great pain and misfortune, he never loses his faith in God.

412   **Suffering the wrongs done to us** "True patience is to suffer the wrongs done to us by others in an unruffled spirit and without feeling resentment. Patience bears with others because

it loves them; to bear with them and yet to hate them is not the virtue of patience but a smokescreen for anger."
POPE ST. GREGORY I, THE GREAT (c. 540–604), ITALY

413 **No anxiety** "Where there is patience and humility, there is neither anger nor vexation."
ST. FRANCIS OF ASSISI (c. 1181–1226), ITALY

414 **A queen** "Patience is the queen of the virtues."
ST. JOHN CHRYSOSTOM (c. 347–407), ASIA MINOR (TURKEY)

415 **Ballast for the storms** "Patience is the ballast of the soul, that will keep it from rolling and tumbling in the greatest storms...."
JOHN HENRY HOPKINS (1792–1868), USA

416 **Time for yourself** "Have patience with all things, but chiefly have patience with yourself. Do not lose courage in considering your own imperfections but instantly set about remedying them—every day begin the task anew."
ST. FRANCIS OF SALES (1567–1622), FRANCE

HUMILITY

417 **Heart of the matter** "The foundation of our [Christian] philosophy is humility."
ST. JOHN CHRYSOSTOM (c. 347–407), ASIA MINOR (TURKEY)

418 **High virtue** "... humility goes before honor."
PROVERBS 15:33

419 **Before God** "Humble yourselves before the Lord, and he will exalt you."
JAMES 4:10

420 **Small things** "The smallest things become great when God requires them of us; they are small only in themselves; they are always great when they are done for God."
FRANÇOIS FÉNELON (1651–1715), FRANCE

421 **Exaltation of the humble** "[A]ll who exalt themselves will be humbled, but all who humble themselves will be exalted."
LUKE 18:14

422 **The long road** "Remember the long way that the Lord your God has led you these forty years in the wilderness, in order to humble you, testing you to know what was in your heart, whether or not you would keep his commandments. He humbled you by letting you hunger, then by feeding you with manna..."
DEUTERONOMY 8:2–3

423 **Like a child** "Whoever becomes humble like this child is the greatest in the kingdom of heaven."
MATTHEW 18:4

---

424 **THE TRIUMPHAL ENTRY INTO JERUSALEM**
The biblical story of Jesus final entry into Jerusalem before his Crucifixion (Mark 11:1–11) is a celebrated event, but it is by no means a militaristic triumph: Jesus chose to ride on a donkey, an animal of burden and often an object of derision. Matthew finds in this the fulfillment of Zechariah's prophecy, "Look, your king is coming to you, humble, and mounted

on a donkey..." (Matthew 21:5). This "king," the son of David, whom the Jews were expecting to defeat their enemies, has not come to conquer anything, apart from people's hearts.

---

425 **Worthless virtues** "Without humility of heart all the other virtues by which one runs toward God seem—and are—absolutely worthless."

ANGELA OF FOLIGNO (1248–1309), ITALY

426 **Truth** "The reason why God is so great a Lover of humility is because He is the great Lover of truth. Now humility is nothing but truth, while pride is nothing but lying."
VINCENT DE PAUL (1580–1660), FRANCE

427 **Hymn of the Passion**
"Let the same mind be in you that was in Christ Jesus,
who, though he was in the form of God,
did not regard equality with God as something to be exploited,

but emptied himself taking the form of a slave,

being born in human likeness.

And being found in human form,

he humbled himself and became obedient to the point of

death—even death on a cross."

PHILIPPIANS 2:5–8

428 THE WASHING OF FEET

At the Last Supper, Jesus "poured water into a basin and began to wash his disciples' feet and to wipe them with the towel..." (John 13:5). Foot-washing was an act of hospitality that was usually undertaken by servants, but in a gesture of humble service, Jesus takes on the role. Although the act also has an association with Christian baptism, Jesus indicates to his disciples that by washing their feet, "I have set you an example." The disciples too should "wash one another's feet" (John 13:14–15).

429   **Meek and gentle** "Take my yoke upon you, and learn from me; for I am gentle and humble in heart, and you will find rest for your souls. For my yoke is easy, and my burden is light."
MATTHEW 11:29–30

430   **Self-knowledge** "Humility is the virtue by which a man recognizes his own unworthiness because he really knows himself."
ST. BERNARD OF CLAIRVAUX (1090–1153), FRANCE

431   **Consideration of others** Early Christians cautioned against arrogance, which it was felt affronted the dignity of others when a follower of Christ should look first to the interests of others. In a somewhat similar vein, Paul urged: **"Do nothing from selfish ambition or conceit, but in humility regard others as better than yourselves" (432)** (Philippians 2:3).

433   **Grace to the humble** "And all of you must clothe yourselves with humility in your dealings with one another, for, 'God opposes the proud, but gives grace to the humble.'"
1 PETER 5:5

434   **Like a bee** "Humility must always be doing its work like a bee making its honey in the hive: without humility all will be lost."
ST. TERESA OF AVILA (1515–1582), SPAIN

435   **Rare thing** "It is no great thing to be humble when you are brought low; but to be humble when you are praised is a great and rare thing."
ST. BERNARD OF CLAIRVAUX (1090–1153), FRANCE

436   **Parable of the banquet** "When you are invited by someone to a wedding banquet, do not sit down at a place of honor, in case someone more distinguished than you has been invited by your host; and the host who invited both of you may come and say to you, 'Give this person your place,' and then in disgrace you would start to take the lowest place. But when you are invited, go and sit at the lowest place, so that when your host comes, he may say to you, 'Friend, move up higher'; then you will be honored....'"
LUKE 14:7–11

437   **Ruinous pride** "Unless humility precede, accompany, and follow

[169]

up all the good we accomplish, unless we keep our eyes fixed on it, pride will snatch everything right out of our hands."
ST. AUGUSTINE OF HIPPO (354–430), NORTH AFRICA

438 **Selfless** "Humility does not mean thinking less of yourself than of other people, nor does it mean having a low opinion of your own gifts. It means freedom from thinking about yourself at all."
WILLIAM TEMPLE (1881–1944), ARCHBISHOP OF CANTERBURY

439 **Inner peace** "Great peace is with the humble man, but in the heart of a proud man are always envy and anger."
THOMAS À KEMPIS (c. 1380–1471), GERMANY

440 **Bringer of wisdom** "When pride comes, then comes disgrace; but with humility comes wisdom."
PROVERBS 11:2

441 **Protected** "If you are humble, nothing will touch you, neither praise nor disgrace, because you know what you are."
MOTHER TERESA (1910–1997), INDIA

442   **The haughty spirit** "Pride goes before destruction, and a haughty spirit before a fall."
PROVERBS 16:18

443   **Path to pleasure** "Obedience is the road to freedom, humility the road to pleasure, unity the road to personality."
C.S. LEWIS (1898–1963), ENGLAND

444   **Merit has its limits** "The sufficiency of my merit is to know that my merit is not sufficient."
ST. AUGUSTINE OF HIPPO (354–430), NORTH AFRICA

445   **Firmest foundation** "True humility—the basis of the Christian system—is the low but deep and firm foundation of all virtues."
EDMUND BURKE (1729–1797), IRELAND

446   **Shining jewel** "Sense shines with a double luster when it is set in humility. An able and yet humble man is a jewel worth a kingdom."
WILLIAM PENN (1644–1718), ENGLAND/USA

447 Have faith Human courage is central to the Christian faith, particularly in the resolution to follow God and to spread his word. But according to the faithful, courage will come directly from God if we place our trust and hope in him: "Be strong, and let your heart take courage, all you who wait for the Lord" (Psalm 31:24; see also 2 Corinthians 3).

448 Essential virtue "Facing the darkness, admitting the pain, allowing the pain to be pain, is never easy. That is why

courage—big-heartedness—is the most essential virtue on the spiritual journey."
MATTHEW FOX (BORN 1940), USA

449 **Stand firm** "Keep alert, stand firm in your faith, be courageous, be strong. Let all that you do be done in love."
1 CORINTHIANS 16:13

450 **Shadow of death** "Yea, though I walk through the valley of the shadow of death, I will fear no evil; for thou art with me."
PSALM 23 [KJV]

451 **God-given strength** "The night is given us to take breath, to pray, to drink deep at the fountain of power. The day, to use the strength which has been given us, to go forth to work with it till the evening."
FLORENCE NIGHTINGALE (1820–1910), ENGLAND

452 **Your daily battles** "The world has no room for cowards. We must all be ready somehow to toil, to suffer, to die. And yours

is not the less noble because no drum beats before you when you go out to your daily battlefields, and no crowds shout your coming when you return from your daily victory and defeat."
ROBERT LOUIS STEVENSON (1850–1894), SCOTLAND

453 DAVID AND GOLIATH

For years the Israelites had struggled to hold their own against the mighty Philistines, among whom was a great warrior, Goliath. When the Israelites saw him, they "were very much afraid" (1 Samuel 17:24). Although a mere shepherd boy, David offered to fight this "champion." When the Israelite king, Saul, protested, David said he would draw on all his courage. As he confronted Goliath, he had total faith in God's guardianship: "You come to me with sword and spear and javelin; but I come to you in the name of the Lord of hosts.... the Lord will deliver you into my hand" (1 Samuel 17:45).

454 **Bold leadership** "Then Moses summoned Joshua and said to him in the sight of all Israel: 'Be strong and bold, for you are the one who will go with this people into the land that the Lord has sworn to their ancestors to give them; and you will put them in possession of it.'"
DEUTERONOMY 31:7

455 **A cardinal virtue** Some Christian scholars identified prudence, justice, temperance, and courage as the four "cardinal virtues" of humankind, upon which all other virtues depend. The medieval theologian St. Thomas Aquinas (1225–1274) declared that "The principal act of courage is to endure and withstand dangers doggedly rather than to attack them."

456 **Sacred war** "The Church knows nothing of the sacredness of war. The Church which prays the 'Our Father' asks God only for peace."
DIETRICH BONHOEFFER (1905–1945), GERMANY

457 **Taking the cross** Brave crusaders who offered to undertake the arduous expedition to recover the Holy Land were said to "take

[175]

the cross." Their vow was fulfilled when they reached the Holy Sepulchre, the traditional site of the tomb of Jesus in Jerusalem.

---

458 **THE LAST SUPPER**
The Last Supper marks the end of Jesus' ministry and the start of his "Passion," or suffering, for which he has to gather immense courage. He gives his disciples bread and wine, which thereafter represent his flesh and blood, sacrificed to redeem humankind—the wine, he declares, is "my blood of the covenant, which is poured out for many for the forgiveness of sins" (Matthew 26:28). In this formal declaration of his messiahship, Jesus says it is the last time they will be together, "before I suffer."

---

459 **Facing our fears** In a moment of great personal distress, knowing that his crucifixion is drawing near, Jesus reveals his human side and doubts his fortitude. For the first time he prays to be released: "My Father, if it is possible, let this cup pass from

me...." (Matthew 26:39). He has to summon courage to yield his destiny into God's hands: "yet not what I want but what you want."

460 **Triumph over doubt** "The courage to be is rooted in the God who appears when God has disappeared in the anxiety of doubt." PAUL TILLICH (1886–1965), USA

461 **Perseverance** "... let us run with perseverance the race that is set before us, looking to Jesus the pioneer and perfecter of our faith, who for the sake of the joy that was set before him endured the cross, disregarding its shame." HEBREWS 12:1–2

462 **World conquest** "In the world you face persecution. But take courage; I have conquered the world!" JOHN 16:33

463 **Fierce tests** In his first letter to

Christians scattered throughout Asia Minor (modern Turkey), the apostle Peter writes of the fear and suffering his communities are facing: "Beloved, do not be surprised at the fiery ordeal that is taking place among you to test you, as though something strange were happening to you. But rejoice insofar as you are sharing Christ's sufferings, so that you may also be glad and shout for joy when his glory is revealed" (1 Peter 4:12–13).

---

464 **KEEPING THE FAITH**

Many early Christians suffered because they were rejected from the Jewish synagogues and refused to worship pagan gods. Keeping the faith required encouragement from Church leaders. Paul wrote to his flock at Corinth explaining that their suffering was not to be taken as a sign of failure. Rather, they must share in the suffering of Christ, "For while we live, we are always being given up to death for Jesus' sake" (2 Corinthians 4:11).

465 **No disgrace** "Yet if any of you suffers as a Christian, do not consider it a disgrace, but glorify God because you bear this name."
1 PETER 4:16

466 **Recognize God's compassion** "God is full of compassion, and never fails those who are afflicted and despised, if they trust in him alone."
ST. TERESA OF AVILA (1515–1582), SPAIN

467 **CHRISTIAN MARTYRS**
The word "martyr," meaning "witness," was used of the apostles, who had witnessed Christ's life and resurrection. As persecution of the early Church spread, the term came to refer to those who suffered for their faith, and eventually to those who died for it. Paul and Peter both perished in Rome and many Christians were thrown to lions in the Coliseum. Early saints were all martyrs, and the late Pope

John Paul II (1978–2005) sanctified many of the faithful who gave their lives in adversity.

---

468   **Stoning** "While they were stoning Stephen, he prayed, 'Lord Jesus, receive my spirit.' Then he knelt down and cried out in a loud voice, 'Lord, do not hold this sin against them.'"
ACTS 7:59

469   **Paul in Rome** "That night the Lord stood near him and said, 'Keep up your courage! For just as you have testified for me in Jerusalem, so you must bear witness also in Rome.'"
ACTS 23:11

470   **Torment** "We hope to suffer torment for our Lord Jesus Christ and so to be saved."
ST. JUSTIN MARTYR (c. 100–c. 165), ASIA MINOR (TURKEY)

471   **Faint?** "When we feel us too bold, remember our own feebleness. When we feel us too faint, remember Christ's strength."
THOMAS MORE (1478–1535), ENGLAND

472 **Moral bravery** "Mere physical courage—the absence of fear—
simply is not worth calling bravery. It's the bravery of the tiger,
not the moral bravery of the man."
ROBERT BENSON (1871–1914), ENGLAND

473 **Three things** "God, give us grace to accept with serenity the things
that cannot be changed, courage to change the things that should
be changed, and the wisdom to distinguish the one from the other."
REINHOLD NIEBUHR (1892–1971), USA

474 **Two daughters** "Hope has two beautiful daughters—their
names are anger and courage; anger at the way things are, and
courage to see that they do not remain the way they are."
ST. AUGUSTINE OF HIPPO (354–430), NORTH AFRICA

475 **Sleep peacefully in your bed** "Have courage for the great
sorrows of life and patience for the small ones; and when you
have laboriously accomplished your daily task, go to sleep in
peace. God is awake."
VICTOR HUGO (1802–1885), FRANCE

DUTY

476   **Reality check** "Our duty as Christians is always to keep heaven in our eye and earth under our feet."
MATTHEW HENRY (1662–1714), ENGLAND

477   **Count not the cost** "To give and not to count the cost, to fight and not to heed the wounds, to toil and not to seek for rest, to labour and to ask for no reward."
ST. IGNATIUS OF LOYOLA (1491–1556), SPAIN

478   **Be responsible** "Action springs not from thought, but from a readiness for responsibility."
DIETRICH BONHOEFFER (1906–1945), GERMANY

479   **Do good**
"Do all the good you can ...
In all the ways you can
In all the places you can
To all the people you can
As long as you can."
JOHN WESLEY (1703–1791), ENGLAND

480 WATCHFULNESS

One of the key stipulations from Christ during his ministry was to be alert and mindful that the kingdom of God could come at any time. Although the Gospels were written with the second coming of Christ in mind, the command has a wider application. Its main focus is on the importance of always putting your best into

whatever you do, and not slacking when you
think no one is looking. The famous example
in the Gospels comes when Jesus goes to pray
in the Garden of Gethsemane (Matthew 26:36–
46). It is a crucial time, when he is about to
be betrayed, and he asks his closest disciples,
Peter, James, and John, to keep watch over him.
But while he is at prayer they fall asleep—not
just once, three times—and the soldiers arrive.
Jesus, ever forgiving, understood human
weakness when he said to them, "the spirit
indeed is willing, but the flesh is weak."

---

481   **Obey God** "Fear God, and keep his commandments; for that is
the whole duty of everyone."
ECCLESIASTES 12:13

482   **A divine command** The German philosopher Immanuel Kant
(1724–1805) stressed the role of duty as a religious imperative.
Although, he says, we cannot know God because our human

minds are not capable of such knowledge, the moral law demands
that we should recognize "all duties as divine commands."

483   **A step in the dark?** "Let us have faith that right makes might;
and in that faith let us to the end, dare to do our duty as we
understand it."
ABRAHAM LINCOLN (1809–1865), USA

484   **Out of love** "A perfect man would never act from a sense of
duty.... Duty is only a substitute for love, like a crutch which is a
substitute for a leg. Most of us need the crutch at times; but of
course it is idiotic to use the crutch when our own legs can do
the journey on their own."
C.S. LEWIS (1898–1963), ENGLAND

485   **Drawing God back into your life** "If you make a god of
your best moments, you will find that God will fade out of
your life and never come back until you do the duty that
lies nearest."
OSWALD CHAMBERS (1874–1917), ENGLAND

486 **Rewarding** "If I proclaim the gospel, this gives me no ground for boasting, for an obligation is laid on me, and woe to me if I do not proclaim the gospel! For, I do this of my own will, I have a reward; but if not of my own will, I am entrusted with a commission."
1 CORINTHIANS 9:16–17

487 **Not necessarily dull** "Duty does not have to be dull. Love can make it beautiful and fill it with life."
THOMAS MERTON (1915–1968), NEW ZEALAND/USA

---

488 **MARY AND MARTHA**
Luke 10:38–42 describes the relationship between two sisters, Mary and Martha, who live with their brother Lazarus. Martha typifies the "active" life, one that is intent on fulfilling duty—in this case, cleaning the house. Her complaint about her sister Mary being lazy is immediately rebuffed by Jesus, who says that Mary's concentration on his words was more important than household chores. The message

is not that contemplation is more important than active service but that there is a time for everything. Martha let herself be "worried and distracted by many things" (10:41), instead of getting her priorities right, as Mary did.

---

489 **Spiritual duty** "Fear is never a good counselor and victory over fear is the first spiritual duty of man."
NIKOLAI BERDYAEV (1874–1948), RUSSIA

490 **Making happy** "Exactness in little duties is a wonderful source of cheerfulness."
FREDERICK FABER (1814–1863), ENGLAND

491 **Lay foundations** "Faithfulness in carrying out present duties is the best preparation for the future."
FRANÇOIS FÉNELON (1651–1715), FRANCE

492 **Pure motives** "In the fulfilment of your duties, let your intentions be so pure that you reject from your actions any other

motive than the glory of God and the salvation of souls."
ST. ANGELA MERICI (1474–1540), ITALY

493   **Be happy** "There is no duty we so much underrate as the duty of being happy."
ROBERT LOUIS STEVENSON (1850–1894), SCOTLAND

494   **Daily sacrifices** "To take up the cross of Christ is no great action done once for all; it consists in the continual practice of small duties which are distasteful to us."
JOHN HENRY NEWMAN (1801–1890), ENGLAND

495   **Only our duty** "So you also, when you have done all that you were ordered to do, say, 'We are worthless slaves; we have done only what we ought to have done!'"
LUKE 17:10

496   **Heaven's command** "Duty—the command of heaven, the eldest voice of God."
CHARLES KINGSLEY (1819–1875), ENGLAND

PRUDENCE

497   NO WORLDLY PROFIT
Worldly prudence aims at financial security
and prosperity. But as the 17th-century French
monk St. Vincent De Paul said, Christian
prudence takes "Incarnate Wisdom for its guide
in every thought, word, and work." The main
principle here is faith, not worldly judgment.
However, prudence always involves correct
judgment in practical matters—we must use
our intellect to recognize the good and evil
possibilities in any situation, and to discern the
appropriate route to take.

---

498   Hindrance and help "Prudence is
love discerning aright that
which helps from that
which hinders us in tending
to God."

ST. AUGUSTINE OF HIPPO (354–430),
NORTH AFRICA

499   **Aforethought** "The simple believe everything, but the clever consider their steps."
PROVERBS 14:15

500   **Think it through** "Prudence is right reason in action."
ST. THOMAS AQUINAS (1225–1274), ITALY

501   **Within your means** "According to her cloth she cut her coat."
JOHN DRYDEN (1631–1700), ENGLAND

502   **Be prepared** One aspect of Christian prudence is the necessity for preparedness. The Gospels, in particular, talk about being prepared for Christ's return to Earth, when all will be judged—Luke's parables of the Watchful Slaves and Matthew's of the Ten Bridesmaids are examples that serve as a general imperative to be ready for any eventuality.

   Light your lamps (503): "Be dressed for action and have your lamps lit; be like those who are waiting for their master to return from the wedding banquet, so that they may open the door for him as soon as he comes and knocks. Blessed are those slaves whom the master finds alert when he comes" (Luke 12:35–37).

The faithful worker (504): "Who then is the faithful and prudent manager whom his master will put in charge of his slaves ...? Blessed is that slave whom his master will find at work when he arrives. Truly I tell you, he will put that one in charge of all his possessions" (Luke 12:42–44).

The parable of the **Ten Bridesmaids (or the Wise and Foolish Virgins) (505)** in Matthew 25:1–13 tells of how five

prudent bridesmaids came to a wedding banquet prepared with lamps and spare oil. The other five bridesmaids, however, took only their lamps. The bridegroom was delayed and the foolish bridesmaids had no oil to relight their lamps. They went out to buy some but in their absence the bridegroom arrived. When the foolish bridesmaids returned, the banquet door was shut.

506   **Right balance** "Live and hope in the Lord and let your service be according to reason. Season your whole offering with the salt of prudence."

ST. CLARE OF ASSISI (c. 1193–1253), ITALY

507   **THE RIGHT SEASON**

In some contexts, Christian prudence can refer to the significance of correct timing in human life. The "wisdom literature" in the Bible, for example, talks about the appropriate time for everything, even things we may not wish to experience. Everything has its place in our lives and must be suffered, just as spring cannot arrive without a winter. The meeting of positives and negatives is a necessary aspect of existence and is ultimately reflected in the symbol of the Cross, in which life meets death and life again.

---

508 **Time and place** "For everything there is a season, and a time for every matter under heaven: a time to be born, and a time to die; a time to plant, and a time to pluck up what is planted; a time to kill, and a time to heal ... a time to weep, and a time to laugh; a time to mourn, and a time to dance ... a time to keep silence, and a time to speak; a time to love, and a time to hate; a time for war, and a time for peace."
ECCLESIASTES 3:1–8

509 **Softly scanning eye**
"The softest breeze to fairest flowers gives birth: Think not that Prudence dwells in dark abodes,
She scans the future with the eye of gods."
WILLIAM WORDSWORTH (1770–1850), ENGLAND

510 RIGHT ACTION

St. Thomas Aquinas (c. 1225–1274) described prudence as the "charioteer of virtues" because it is the cause and measure of all moral virtues. For example, a person can only live in temperance once he or she has acquired the ability to assess the right actions to take when confronted by instinctual cravings. Aquinas believed that by weighing up the best course of action in such situations, one acquires "the perfected ability to make right decisions."

---

511 Is it of God? "We must not trust every word of others or feeling within ourselves, but cautiously and patiently try the matter, to see whether it is of God."
THOMAS À KEMPIS (c. 1380–1471), GERMANY

512 With lightness of step "What you hold, may you always hold. What you do, may you always do and never abandon. But with swift pace, light step, and unswerving feet ... go forward securely,

joyfully and swiftly on the path of prudent happiness."
ST. CLARE OF ASSISI (c. 1193–1253), ITALY

513 **Think first** "Prudence must precede every action that we
undertake; for, if prudence be wanting, there is nothing,
however good it may seem, which is not turned into evil."
ST. BASIL THE GREAT (c. 330–379), ASIA MINOR (TURKEY)

514 **Root of all evil** In his letter to Timothy, Paul warns of the perils
of becoming obsessed with making money, for "the love of
money is a root of all kinds of evil" (1 Timothy 6:10).

515 **Choose your words** "A word fitly spoken is like apples of gold
in a setting of silver."
PROVERBS 25:11

516 **Spare your breath** "Never be rash with your mouth, nor let
your heart be quick to utter a word before God, for God is in
heaven, and you upon earth; therefore let your words be few."
ECCLESIASTES 5:2

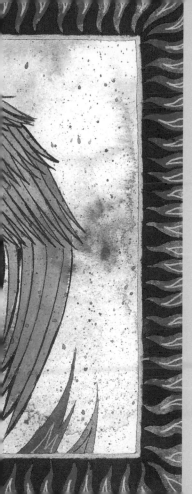

Faith & Hope

Messages of the Prophets   200

The Ministry of Jesus   209

Teachings on Faith   217

Prayer   227

Miracles   239

Inspiration   249

Doubt   255

Freedom   263

MESSAGES OF THE PROPHETS

517 THE VOICE OF DIVINE WILL
The biblical prophets were ancient Israelites
called upon by God to speak on his behalf (the
word "prophet" is derived from the Hebrew,
nabi, meaning spokesperson). Although
their primary role was to ensure a healthy
relationship between God and the nation, they
also possessed the power to foretell the future.

518 **God's speakers** "Long ago God spoke to our ancestors in many and various ways by the prophets."
HEBREWS 1:1

519 **Stand firm**
"Do not be afraid ...
For I [the Lord] am with you to deliver you."
JEREMIAH 1:8

520 **Burning fire** The prophet Jeremiah was faced with the daunting task of informing the Israelites that their beloved city would fall to the Babylonians. He could no longer delay his God-given duty to tell the people, even though he knew he would suffer their wrath, for "within me there is something like a burning fire shut up in my bones" (Jeremiah 20:9). Only by facing up to the truth and accepting it can we live with our consciences.

521 **Harbingers of hope** "The Old Testament prophets were more than statesmen and social reformers.... Prediction was an integral element of their message.... But they were not pessimists. They

believed ... that beyond the
immediate future there was a
brighter age that should see
God's will perfectly done."
H.H. ROWLEY (1890–1969),
ENGLAND

522   **Valley of bones** In a
breathtaking episode, the prophet
Ezekiel is shown a valley full of
the bones of dead animals. To
his amazement, the bones begin
to come alive. The message not only gives hope to the homeless
Israelites (Ezekiel 37:11), but is also a divine promise of life after
death: "I will put my spirit within you, and you shall live" (37:14).

523   **Recognize God's wishes** "[W]hat does the Lord require of
you but to do justice, and to love kindness, and to walk humbly
with your God?"
MICAH 6:8

524   **The soul that seeks** The prophet Jeremiah frequently cries out to God with a sense of abandonment. When his hopes are dashed repeatedly, "with eyes a fountain of tears" (Jeremiah 9:1), he resorts to outright protest. Yet he knows in his heart that "the Lord is good to those who wait for him, to the soul that seeks him" (Lamentations 3:25).

---

525   **THE MESSIAH**
The idea of a future deliverer of Israel in the person of a messiah was present at the time of the prophet Isaiah, who voiced the hopes of his people. The Messiah, thought to be a divinely appointed king descended from David, would become the vessel by which God's blessings poured out upon his beloved people.

---

526   **Enlightenment** "The prophets did not speak on their own accord, but were enlightened by God, to see those things which they themselves would not have otherwise been able to understand."
JOHN CALVIN (1509–1564), FRANCE/SWITZERLAND

527 **Power of the prophet** "Those who speak in a tongue build up themselves, but those who prophesy build up the church."
1 CORINTHIANS 14:4

528 **Advice** "Seek good and not evil."
AMOS 5:14

529 **God's inspiration** "The prophets ... being filled with the inspiration of the one God ... predicted things to come, with ... harmonious voice."
LUCIUS LACTANTIUS (c. 240–c. 320), NORTH AFRICA

530 **Guiding stars** "Every cycle has its prophets as guiding stars; and they are burning candles ... to light the spiritual temple on earth.... When they have done their work, they will pass away; but the candlesticks will remain, and other lights will be placed in them."
ANTOINETTE DOOLITTLE (1810–1886), USA

531 **Like mysticism today** "The only satisfactory parallel to the

prophetic experience is the phenomena of mysticism ... [mystics] affirm that the immediate experience of God is ineffable; like the prophets, they must employ imagery and symbolism to describe it."
J.L. MCKENZIE (1910–2008), USA

532   **Seeking justice** "... remove the evil of your doings from before my eyes; cease to do evil, learn to do good; seek justice, rescue the oppressed, defend the orphan, plead for the widow."
ISAIAH 1:16–17

533   **Royal indulgence** The prophet Amos railed at the astounding indulgence of the royals. Instead of using its wealth to help the poor, King Ahab's court squandered it on fine living: they "lie on beds of ivory ... drink wine from bowls, and anoint themselves with the finest oils" (Amos 6:4–6). Amos, a herdsman, foresees the day when this "Ivory House"

(1 Kings 22:39) will pass away as a consequence of its greed, pride, and complacency.

534   JONAH AND THE FISH
The biblical story of the prophet Jonah and the fish mirrors the death and resurrection of Christ. To save his fellow sailors from a tempest, Jonah jumps off the boat, taking the life-threatening storm with him. God sends a large fish to swallow him up, thus saving him. The period Jonah spent inside the fish's belly recalls the time Christ spent in hell following the Crucifixion and before his resurrection.
But in the same way as Jesus was resurrected, so the "Lord spoke to the fish, and it spewed Jonah out upon the dry land" (Jonah 2:10).

535   Certainty "For I know that my Redeemer lives, and that at the last he will stand upon the earth; and after my skin has been thus destroyed, then in my flesh I shall see God, whom I shall see on my side, and my eyes shall behold, and not another."

JOB 19:25–27

536   **Joy again** "In this place of which you say, 'It is a waste' ...
there shall once more be heard the voice of mirth and the voice
of gladness."

JEREMIAH 33:10–11

537   **Jesus the prophet** There are numerous references in the Bible
indicating that Jesus was considered by many to be a prophet,
delivering divine messages of hope and faith direct from God.
Luke (24:19) describes him as **"a prophet mighty in deed
and word" (538)**, while Peter (Acts 2: 22) notes how, through
him, God performs **"deeds of power, wonders, and signs"
(539)**. On entering Jerusalem, he is announced as **"Jesus, the
prophet of Nazareth of Galilee" (540)**. Some scholars have
also identified Jesus as the special prophet mentioned in Moses'
prediction that, **"The Lord your God will raise up for you a
prophet like me from among your own people (541)**; you
shall heed such a prophet" (Deuteronomy 18:15).

THE MINISTRY OF JESUS

542   **Eternal life** "But whosoever drinketh of the water that I shall give him shall never thirst; but the water that I shall give him shall be in him a well of water springing up into everlasting life."
JOHN 4:14 [KJV]

543   **Belief** "All things can be done for the one who believes."
MARK 9:23

544   **Only believe** "Have faith in God.... whatever you ask for in prayer, believe that you have received it, and it will be yours."
MARK 11:22–25

545   **Eternal life** "For God so loved the world that he gave his only begotten Son, that whosoever believeth in him should not perish, but have everlasting life."
JOHN 3:16 [KJV]

546   **Teacher's guide** "Preach the Gospel at all times, and when necessary use words."
ST. FRANCIS OF ASSISI (c. 1182–1226), ITALY

547 SERMON ON THE MOUNT

Jesus' famous Sermon on the Mount (Matthew 5–7) offers a vision of life in God's kingdom. Earthly values are often turned upside down, as in the command, "love your enemies" (Matthew 5:44). Only if we have faith in Christ will we be able to meet its challenging demands. Jesus exhorts his followers: "be perfect as your heavenly Father" (Matthew 5:48).

---

548 The Beatitudes At the beginning of his Sermon on the Mount, Jesus delivered the Beatitudes (Matthew 5:3–12), or "Blessings," which focus on the virtues that will ensure entry into the kingdom of heaven: **"Blessed are the poor in spirit (549)**, for theirs is the kingdom of heaven;" **"Blessed are those who mourn (550)**, for they will be comforted;" **"Blessed are the meek (551)**, for they will inherit the earth;" **"Blessed are those who hunger and thirst for righteousness (552)**, for they will be filled;" **"Blessed are the merciful (553)**, for they will receive mercy;" **"Blessed are the pure in heart (554)**, for

they will see God;" **"Blessed are the peacemakers (555)**, for they will be called children of God;" **"Blessed are those who are persecuted for righteousness' sake (556)**, for theirs is the kingdom of heaven;" **"Blessed are you when people revile you and persecute you and utter all kinds of evil against you falsely, on my account (557).** Rejoice and be glad, for your reward is great in heaven...."

558   **New Moses** In stressing he has not "come to abolish the law but to fulfill" it (Matthew 5:17), Jesus meant that the law of Moses (the Commandments) is brought to fruition in his gospel. People must examine their inner motives and attitudes as well as observing good behavior. Only then will we be able to live the Law of Moses in the spirit of love that Jesus intended.

559   **Let your light shine brightly** If you do something good, do not be modest and keep quiet about your efforts. As Jesus said, "No one after lighting a lamp puts it under the bushel basket, but on the lampstand, and it gives light to all in the house" (Matthew 5:15).

560 **THE PARABLES**
"With many such parables he spoke the word to them" (Mark 4:33). Jesus' parables often take the form of riddles that require thought before their meaning becomes clear. They sometimes challenge attitudes and assumptions, shocking listeners out of their complacency; some give insight into the nature of the kingdom of God, and others highlight moral responsibilities.

---

561 **Materialism** Jesus often warned of the perils of desiring possessions: **"Be on your guard against all kinds of greed (562)**; for one's life does not consist in the abundance of possessions" (Luke 12:15). And again, in the Sermon on the Mount, he advises, **"Do not store up for yourselves treasures on earth (563)** ... but store up treasures for yourselves in heaven.... For where your treasure is, there your heart will be also" (Matthew 6:19–21).

564 **Cost of discipleship** "Whoever does not carry the cross and

follow me cannot be my disciple. For which of you, intending to build a tower, does not first sit down and estimate the cost, to see whether he has enough to complete it?'"
LUKE 14:27–30

565 **God or Mammon** "No one can serve two masters; for a slave will either hate the one and love the other, or be devoted to the one and despise the other. You cannot serve God and wealth."
MATTHEW 6:24

566 **Easier route** "It is easier for a camel to go through the eye of a needle than for someone who is rich to enter the kingdom of God."
MATTHEW 19:24

567 **A rich man and Lazarus** Jesus was appalled at the rich–poor divide, and one parable (Luke 16:19–31) tells of Lazarus, a poor man, who dies and goes to heaven. A rich man who also dies finds himself in hell; he asks Abraham if a warning can be sent to his brothers so that they might avoid his torment. Abraham replies that they already have guides in the prophets to the conduct required by God, yet they are indifferent—they "look but do not perceive" (Mark 4:12), as Jesus said on another occasion.

568 **Sowing seeds** Just as a farmer who scatters seed on the ground does not know how it grows night and day, "of its own accord the land produces" (Mark 4:28), so the kingdom of God comes without human effort.

569 **The promise** "Ask, and it will be given you; search, and you will find; knock, and the door will be opened for you."
MATTHEW 7:7

570 **Be calm** "Do not let your hearts be troubled. Believe in God, believe also in me [Jesus]."
JOHN 14:1

[215]

571   **The way** "I am the way, and the truth, and the life. No one comes to the Father except through me. If you know me, you will know my Father also."
JOHN 14:6–7

572   **Examine your conscience** The Pharisees challenged Jesus to defy the biblical teaching that adulterous women should be sentenced to death. Jesus said, "Let anyone among you who is without sin be the first to throw a stone at her" (John 8:7).

573   **Think only of today** "Do not worry about tomorrow, for tomorrow will bring worries of its own."
MATTHEW 6:34

574   **Good shepherd** Jesus likened himself to the good shepherd who "lays down his life for his sheep" (John 10:11). In the same way, Jesus, as Christ, sacrificed his own life to save humankind.

575   **Continuity** John's gospel reveals that after Jesus' departure from Earth, the "Spirit of truth" will enter his disciples (John 14:17).

TEACHINGS ON FAITH

576 **Understanding follows belief** "Faith seeks, understanding finds. This is why the prophet says, 'Unless you believe, you will not understand' [Isaiah 7:9]."
ST. AUGUSTINE OF HIPPO (354–430), NORTH AFRICA

577 **Understanding** "Now faith is the assurance of things hoped for, the conviction of things not seen."
HEBREWS 11:1

578 **The way to God** "Say to yourself, 'I am loved by God more than I can either conceive or understand.' Let this fill all your soul and never leave you. You will see that this is the way to find God."
HENRI DE TOURVILLE (1842–1903), FRANCE

579 **In hope we are saved** The suffering in the world should not make us despair because "creation was subjected to futility ... in the hope that the creation itself will be set free from its bondage to decay." As recipients of the "first fruits of the Spirit" we "groan inwardly while we wait for adoption" and "wait for it with patience" (Romans 8:18–25).

580   **Believe in your heart** "If you confess with your lips that Jesus is Lord and believe in your heart that God raised him from the dead, you will be saved."
ROMANS 10:9–10

581   **The Roman centurion** The story of the conversion of the Roman centurion Cornelius by Peter is an example of how all faiths are respected by God. Cornelius was a pagan, but a sincere and devout worshipper who "prayed constantly to God" (Acts 10:2). He, and all those who believe in God, whatever their faith, will be accepted by God.

582   **CHRIST'S RETURN**
The early Christian communities believed Christ's return would be imminent. But as the apostle James (5:7) said, "Be patient." Paul insisted the day of the Lord might come any time, like "a thief in

the night" (1 Thessalonians 5:2). The church should not be alarmed at the delay, for as Peter declared, "with the Lord one day is like a thousand years, and a thousand years like one day." (2 Peter 3:8). Christians must maintain their hope undimmed.

---

583 **All-consuming faith** "Faith is the beginning of that which is eternal."
JOHN HENRY NEWMAN (1801–1890), ENGLAND

584 **Open your mind** "To us also, through every star, through every blade of grass, is not God made visible if we will open our minds and our eyes."
THOMAS CARLYLE (1795–1881), SCOTLAND

585 **Glimpses** "Our faith comes in moments. Yet there is a depth in those brief moments which constrains us to ascribe more reality to them than to all other experiences."
RALPH WALDO EMERSON (1803–1882), USA

586 **No test too great** "God is faithful, and he will not let you be
tested beyond your strength, but with the testing he will also
provide the way out so that you may be able to endure it."
1 CORINTHIANS 10:13

587 **Love, hope, faith**
"There is no love without hope,
No hope without love,
And neither hope nor love without faith."
ST. AUGUSTINE OF HIPPO (354–430), NORTH AFRICA

588 **Expanding love** "O how glorious our Faith is! Instead of
restricting hearts, as the world fancies, it uplifts them and
enlarges their capacity to love, to love with an almost infinite
love, since it will continue unbroken beyond our mortal life."
ST. TERESA OF LISIEUX (1873–1897), FRANCE

589 **Actions follow faith** In his epistle, James asked what good was
faith without "works" (good deeds) to show for it? He points to
Abraham's supreme demonstration of his faith in God "when he

offered his son Isaac on the altar". His "faith was active along with his works". Although the essence of the gospel is faith in Christ, "faith is brought to completion by the works" (James 2:14–22).

590   **By God's grace alone** We are unable to save ourselves. As it is written in the epistle to the Ephesians, "By grace you have been saved through faith". But this is "not your own doing; it is the gift of God" (Ephesians 2:8–10).

591   **Mere seeking** "Without faith it is impossible to please God, for whoever would approach him must believe that he exists and that he rewards those who seek him."
HEBREWS 11:6

592   **Nature of faith** "Faith knows nothing of external guarantees.... To demand guarantees and proofs of faith is to fail to understand its very nature by denying the free, heroic act which it inspires."
NIKOLAI BERDYAEV (1874–1948), RUSSIA

593   **Pascal's wager** "It makes more sense to believe in God than to

not believe. If you believe, and God exists, you will be rewarded in the afterlife. If you do not believe, and He exists, you will be punished for your disbelief. If He does not exist, you have lost nothing either way."
BLAISE PASCAL (1623–1662), FRANCE

594 Hymn of Holiness
"Ready for all thy perfect will,
My acts of faith and love repeat,
Till death thy endless mercies seal,
And make the sacrifice complete."
CHARLES WESLEY (1707–1788), ENGLAND

595 Nurture your faith "Faith is kept alive in us, and gathers strength, more from practice than from speculations."
JOSEPH ADDISON (1672–1719), ENGLAND

596 Hope rests on faith "O man, believe in God with all your might, for hope rests on faith, love on hope, and victory on love."
MOTHER JULIAN OF NORWICH (1342–c. 1416), ENGLAND

597   Awe "Faith is awe in the presence of the divine incognito."
KARL BARTH (1886–1968), SWITZERLAND

598   No refuge from life
"Faith is not a refuge from
reality. It is a demand that
we face reality, with all its
difficulties, opportunities,
and implications."
EVELYN UNDERHILL
(1875–1941), ENGLAND

599   Luther's assurance "Ask a
Christian by what work he is
made worthy of the name
of Christian and he can give
no answer but hearing the
word of God, which is faith.
So the ears alone are the
organs of a Christian man,

because he is justified and judged as Christian not by the works of any other part but by faith."
MARTIN LUTHER (1483–1546), GERMANY

600 **Value of faith** "For what can be the value of faith without works [deeds], or works which are not united with the merit of our Lord Jesus Christ?
ST. TERESA OF AVILA (1515–1582), SPAIN

601 **Sense of life** "Faith is the sense of life, that sense by virtue of which man does not destroy himself, but continues to live on. It is the force whereby we live."
LEO TOLSTOY (1828–1910), RUSSIA

602 **In a secular world** "God would have us know that we must live as men who manage our lives without him.... He is weak and powerless in the world, and that is precisely the way [he] ... helps us. Matthew 8:17 makes it quite clear that Christ helps us, not by virtue of his omnipotence, but by ... his weakness and suffering."
DIETRICH BONHOEFFER (1906–1945), GERMANY

603 **Shadows and light**

"The gloom of the world is but a shadow.

Behind it, yet within reach, is joy."

FRA GIOVANNI GIOCONDO (c. 1433–1515), ITALY

604 **Loving care**

"The same loving Father

who cares for you today

Will care for you tomorrow

And everyday."

ST. FRANCIS OF SALES (1567–1622), FRANCE

605 **No excuse to be idle** "We must take care lest, by exalting the merit of faith ... we furnish people with a pretext for relaxing in the practice of good works [deeds]."

ST. IGNATIUS OF LOYOLA (1491–1556), SPAIN

606 **Promise in nature** "Our Lord has written the promise of the resurrection not in books alone, but in every leaf in springtime."

MARTIN LUTHER (1483–1546), GERMANY

607 **God's lead** The English churchman John Henry Newman (1801–1890) claimed our predicaments can provide God with an opportunity to show us the way forward in life and speaks of the trust we need to have: "Keep thou my feet, I do not ask to see The distant scene, one step enough for me."

608 **Beyond reason** "The heart has its reasons of which reason knows nothing."
BLAISE PASCAL (1623–1662), FRANCE

609 **A message** "Do not let loyalty and faithfulness forsake you; bind them around your neck, write them on the tablet of your heart."
PROVERBS 3:3

610 **The vital artery** "Faith is the vital artery of the soul."
THOMAS WATSON (1620–1696), ENGLAND

611 **Three acts** "There are three acts of faith; assent, acceptance, and assurance. "
JOHN FLAVEL (1628–1691), ENGLAND

PRAYER

612   **Find peace** "Stand in awe, and sin not: commune with your own heart, and in your chamber, and be still."
PSALM 4, BOOK OF COMMON PRAYER (1662), ENGLAND

---

613   **THE LORD'S PRAYER**
"The Lord's Prayer," or "Our Father," is Christianity's most famous prayer and forms an integral part of liturgy in all denominations. Its imperatives are beautifully concise and together encapsulate the full force of Jesus' gospel. As the theologian F.D. Maurice (1805–1872) observed, "The Lord's Prayer may be committed to memory quickly, but it is slowly learnt by heart."

---

614   **Putting the past behind us**
A nourishing element of prayer is ridding one's mind of things past that have caused anxiety.

The French monk St. Bernard of Clairvaux (1090–1153) advises us to "forget what is past, rest wholly in the expectation of what is promised ... for what is promised is eternal."

615 **In private** Some of our most important prayers are said on our own. Jesus told his disciples to pray in the quiet of their rooms, "and pray to your Father who is in secret" (Matthew 6:6).

616 **Inner cell** Part of the art of prayer is finding a certain place, posture and, above all, inner disposition that suits you. As St. Catherine of Siena (1347–1380) advised, "Build yourself a cell in your heart and retire there to pray."

617 **Take heart** "Be strong, do not fear! Here is your God."
ISAIAH 35:4

618 **Selfless prayer** If our prayers are designed simply to further our own pleasure, they may not be answered. But John the evangelist insists that, "if we ask anything according to his will, he hears us" (1 John 5:14).

619 **St. Benedict's prayer** "O gracious and Holy Father, give us wisdom to perceive thee; intelligence to understand thee; diligence to seek thee; patience to wait for thee; eyes to behold thee; a heart to meditate upon thee; and a life to proclaim thee." ST. BENEDICT OF NURSIA (c. 480–c. 547), ITALY

620 **Creed** "We believe in one God, the Father almighty, maker of all things visible and invisible; And in one Lord Jesus Christ, the Son of God, begotten of the Father, that is from the substance of the Father. He is God from God, light from light, true God from true God, begotten not made, of one substance with the Father. By him all things were made, things in heaven and on earth." COUNCIL OF NICAEA (AD 325)

621 **In troubled times** Paul taught his church at Corinth to pray to "... the God of all consolation, who consoles us in all our affliction, so that we may be able to console those who are in any affliction with the consolation with which we ourselves are consoled by God" (2 Corinthians 1:3–4).

622   Look to heaven "For me, prayer is a surge of the heart; it is a simple look turned toward heaven, it is a cry of recognition and of love, embracing both trial and joy."
ST. TERESA OF LISIEUX (1873–1897), FRANCE

623   Fervent yearning "No matter how carefully our inner progress is ordered, nothing will come of it unless by God's help. And this is available to those who seek it from the heart, humbly and devoutly; which means ... yearning for it in fervent prayer."
BONAVENTURE (1221–1274), ITALY

624   Beginner's effort "All the beginner in prayer has to do ... is to labour and be resolute and prepare himself with all possible diligence to bring his will into conformity with the will of God."
ST. TERESA OF AVILA (1515–1582), SPAIN

625   PARABLE OF THE UNJUST JUDGE
To encourage his disciples, Jesus told a parable about a widow who pleaded relentlessly for justice from an atheist judge (Luke 18:1–8). Despite his indifference to her cause, he eventually gave in. How much more readily will the Lord answer the cries of his people. Those in need should be patient and, as Luke points out, "pray always and [do] not ... lose heart."

---

626   Unseen power "Pray inwardly, even though you feel no joy in it. For it does good, though you feel nothing, see nothing, yes, even though you think you cannot pray."
MOTHER JULIAN OF NORWICH (1342–c. 1416), ENGLAND

627   My covenant with You "Lord, I am no longer my own, but Yours. Put me to what You will.... Let be employed by You or laid aside for You.... Let me have all things, let me have nothing.... You are mine and I am Yours. So be it. Amen.
JOHN WESLEY (1703–1791), ENGLAND

628   **Prayer for spiritual illumination** "Lord, shed upon our darkened souls the brilliant light of your wisdom so that we may be enlightened and serve you with renewed purity."

ST. EPHRAEM SYRUS (c. 306–373), SYRIA

629   **Hear me** "Hear my prayer, O Lord, Give ear to my supplications! Answer me in Your faithfulness, in Your righteousness!"

PSALM 143:1

630   **God's instrument** "Prayer is a mighty instrument, not for getting man's will done in Heaven, but for getting God's will done in earth."

WILLIAM LAW (1686–1761), ENGLAND

631   **The incense of prayer** "When the Spirit has come to reside in someone, that person cannot stop praying.... the incense of prayer will ascend spontaneously from his heart.... His thoughts

will be prompted by God. The slightest stirring of his heart is like a voice which sings in silence and in secret to the Invisible."
ISAAC OF NINEVEH (7th CENTURY), SYRIA

632 **Give thanks** "In every address to God we must express a grateful regard to him as our benefactor."
MATTHEW HENRY (166–1714), ENGLAND

633 **Weapon against the devil** "Prayer is more powerful than all the devils."
ST. BERNARD OF CLAIRVAUX (1090–1153), FRANCE

634 **Wishes**
"Every wish
Is like a prayer—with God."
ELIZABETH BARRETT BROWNING (1806–1861), ENGLAND

635 **Don't gabble** Jesus advised us not to "heap up empty phrases" (Matthew 6:7) when we pray. In the same vein, St. Edmund the Martyr (c. 840–869) observed, **"I would rather say five**

words devoutly with my heart (636) than five thousand which my soul does not relish with affection and understanding."

637 **Quiet contemplation** "In meditation I heard the Lord say, 'I accept all your prayers whether you speak them, think in your heart, read, or listen to reading but you are much closer to me when you sit quietly in contemplation.'"
MARGERY KEMPE (1373–1439), ENGLAND

638 **Sign of devotion** "The prayer of the mind is not perfect until he no longer realizes himself or the fact that he is praying."
ST. ANTHONY OF EGYPT (251–356)

639 **God stoops** "When I bow to God, God stoops to me."
ROBERT CLEAVER CHAPMAN (1803–1902), ENGLAND

640 **Make us bold** When the apostles Peter and John were arrested for preaching the resurrection, their friends prayed to Christ, to "grant to your servants to speak your word with all boldness, while you stretch out your hand to heal" (Acts 4:29–30).

641   **The greatest success** "He prayeth best, who loveth best."
SAMUEL COLERIDGE (1772–1834), ENGLAND

642   **Essential act** "I have so much to do that I spend several hours in prayer before I am able to do it."
JOHN WESLEY (1703–1791), ENGLAND

643   **The greater work** "Prayer does not fit us for the greater work, prayer is the greater work."
OSWALD CHAMBERS (1874–1917), SCOTLAND

644   **Beginnings** "It is useful to begin everything with prayer, because thereby we surrender ourselves to God and unite ourselves to Him."
PSEUDO-DIONYSIUS THE AREOPAGITE (c. 500), ASIA MINOR (TURKEY)

645   **THE GARDEN OF GETHSEMANE**
The desperation Jesus feels before his arrest and Crucifixion is evident in his prayer to the Father in the garden of Gethsemane—"I am

deeply grieved, even to death" (Mark 14:32). He acknowledges his fear, and his human frailty is more evident here than in any other part of the gospel. He nevertheless expresses his resolve in echoing the Lord's Prayer: "[R]emove this cup from me: yet, not what I want, but what you want" (Mark 14:36).

---

646   **Be still and let God speak** "The very best and utmost of attainment in this life is to remain still and let God act and speak in thee."
MEISTER ECKHART (1260–1327), GERMANY

647   **Rewards** "What we win by prayer we may wear with comfort, and must wear with praise."
MATTHEW HENRY (1662–1714), ENGLAND

648   **With heart** "In prayer it is better to have a heart without words than words without a heart."
JOHN BUNYAN (1628–1688), ENGLAND

649 **Gradual awakening** "A man prayed, and at first he thought that prayer was talking. But he became more quiet until in the end he realized that prayer is listening."

SØREN KIERKEGAARD (1813–1855), DENMARK

---

650 **HAIL MARY**

The "Hail Mary" is a Roman Catholic prayer to the Virgin Mary, based on the Annunciation—the revelation by the archangel Gabriel to Mary of the imminent birth of the Son of God. The faithful count beads on a rosary to help them repeat the fifteen parts of the prayer.

---

651 **The power of a mother's prayers** "St. Anselm tells us that salvation is occasionally more obtained by calling on the name of Mary than by invoking that of Jesus. This is not because He is not the source and Lord of all graces, but because, when we have recourse to the Mother, and she prays for us, her prayers—the prayers of a mother—are more irresistible than our own."

ST. ALPHONSUS LIGUORI (1696–1787), ITALY

MIRACLES

652 **Signs** John the evangelist uses the term "sign" when referring to Jesus' miracles: "... many people saw the miraculous signs he was doing and believed in his name" (2:23). In the gospels, miracles are visible signs of the invisible truth. Whether turning water into wine at the wedding of Cana, walking on water, or the raising of Lazarus, they all point to the transforming miracle for humanity of the death and resurrection of Christ.

653 **Only with God** "No man can do these miracles that thou doest, except God be with him."
JOHN 3:2 [KJV]

654 **That you might believe** "But these [miracles] are written so that you may come to believe that Jesus is the Messiah, the Son of God, and that through believing you may have life in his name."
JOHN 20:31

---

655 **FEEDING THE 5,000**
In the famous miracle of the feeding of the 5,000, Jesus showed that if people who have

more than they need give to those who have nothing, then there will always be enough to go round. Having just five barley loaves and two fishes with which to feed the masses who had come to witness his miraculous cures, Jesus "blessed and broke the loaves ... and all ate and were filled" (Mark 6:41–42).

---

656   **Gifts of the Spirit** "... God added his testimony by signs and wonders and various miracles, and by gifts of the Holy Spirit, distributed according to his will."
HEBREWS 2:4

657   **Do you really need miracles?** "There is in every miracle a silent chiding of the world, and a tacit reprehension of them who require, or who need miracles."
JOHN DONNE (1571–1631), ENGLAND

658   **Daniel and the lions** When the prophet Daniel was placed in a den of hungry lions, so powerful was his spirit that even those most fearsome of creatures would not dare to harm this man "because he had trusted in his God" (Daniel 6:23).

659 **Fall of Jericho** The Old Testament book of Joshua describes the famous siege of Jericho (2:1–22; 6:1–27). Miraculously, a blast on a ram's horn signals the destruction of the city's walls and subsequent capture of the occupying enemy. The divine

intervention shows that even in war, God rewards those who remain steadfast in their devotion. As the author of the epistle to the Hebrews writes, "By faith the walls of Jericho fell after they had been encircled for seven days" (Hebrews 11:30).

660   **All is possible** "Faith will move mountains" is a familiar term. Jesus said a similar thing to his disciples: "He that believeth on me, the works that I do shall he do also" (John 14:12–14 [KJV]). With faith, the laws of the natural world are no barrier to God.

---

661   **RAISING LAZARUS**
There are three biblical accounts of Jesus bringing people back to life. The most famous is that of Lazarus, who was raised from the dead after lying for four days in a cave tomb. Jesus cried out to him, "'Lazarus come out!' The dead man came out...." (John 11:43–44). The incident prefigures Jesus' own death and resurrection, and serves to reawaken faith, demonstrating his power as the Son of God,

sent to Earth to reveal God's glory:
"I am the resurrection and the life. Those
who believe in me, even though they die,
will live" (11:25).

---

662   **Restoring life** "He [Elijah] stretched himself upon the child three times ... and said, 'O Lord my God, I pray thee, let this child's soul come into him again. And the Lord heard the voice of Elijah; and the soul of the child came into him again, and he revived."
1 KINGS 17:21–22 [KJV]

663   **Change** "I never have any difficulty believing in miracles, since I experienced the miracle of a change in my own heart."
ST. AUGUSTINE OF HIPPO (354–430), NORTH AFRICA

664   **I am a miracle** "It is not necessary for me to go far afield in search of miracles. I am a miracle myself. My physical birth and my soul's existence are miracles. First and foremost, the fact that I was even born is a miracle."
TOYOHIKO KAGAWA (1888–1960), JAPAN

665   **CALMING THE STORM**
Our faith is often tested in times of
vulnerability, as evident when Jesus and his
followers take a boat across the Sea of Galilee
(Matthew 8:23–27). In the grip of a sudden
storm, the disciples fear for their lives. The
sea and the storm represent the world and its
adversity; the boat is the church with Christ
at its head. Having subdued the storm, Christ
scolds his students gently, "O ye of little faith."

---

666   **Without aid** "The spirit and meaning of Christ are present and
perceptible to us even without the aid of miracles."
CARL JUNG (1871–1961), SWITZERLAND

667   **Plagues of Egypt** The book of Exodus recounts how God sent a
series of plagues to punish the Egyptians for their imprisonment
of the Israelites, but each time the pharaoh broke his promise to
relent. The first "wonders" (Exodus 11:10) were frogs, gnats, and
flies, which the Egyptians explained away as the result of natural

phenomena. But the punishments worsened. Only with the final one of death to the Egyptians' eldest children (which had no natural explanation) were the Israelites freed. Faith, not demands for supernatural proof, is what God wishes from his people.

668 **Burning bush** Moses encountered God in the desert: "There the angel of the Lord appeared to him in a flame of fire out of a bush ... the bush was blazing, yet it was not consumed.... Moses hid his face, for he was afraid to look at God" (Exodus 3:2–6).

669 **Healing at the Pool of Siloam** For thirty-eight years a disabled man waited patiently by a pool at Jerusalem in the hope of gaining access to its curative waters—but having no assistance, others would push before him. His tremendous faith and perseverance were eventually rewarded by Jesus, who told him, "Stand up, take your mat and walk" (John 5:2–9).

670 **Laying on of hands** A ritual component of healing in ancient Palestine was laying hands on the sick. In Mark's gospel, it is said that Jesus "laid his hands on a few sick people and cured them"

(6:5). He did so not only out of pity for the sick, but because, by working these miracle cures, onlookers might believe he really was the expected messiah.

671 **Beyond reason** "Were the works of God readily understandable by human reason, they would be neither wonderful nor unspeakable."
THOMAS À KEMPIS (c. 1380–1471), GERMANY

672 **Wonderful works** "Glory in his holy name; let the hearts of those who seek the Lord rejoice. Seek the Lord and his strength, seek his presence continually. Remember the wonderful works he has done, his miracles, and the judgments he uttered...."
CHRONICLES 16:10–12

673 **Banishing sickness and evil** "God did extraordinary miracles through Paul, so that when the handkerchiefs or aprons that had touched his skin were brought to the sick, their diseases left them, and the evil spirits came out of them."
ACTS OF THE APOSTLES 19:11–12

INSPIRATION

674   **Reaching for God** From ancient times, tall structures have often represented human attempts to receive divine inspiration. In the Old Testament, a ziggurat (stepped temple), known as the Tower of Babel, was built, "with its top in the heavens" (Genesis 11:4).

675   **From Christ** "We can find no greater inspiration to love even our enemies as brothers and sisters ... than grateful remembrance of Christ's wonderful patience."
ST. AELRED OF RIEVEAULX (c. 1109–c. 1167), ENGLAND

676   **Inspiration of the word** Devotional writer and poet St. Ephraem (c. 306–373) was renowned in the ancient Syrian church for his ascetic life. He wrote many inspiring hymns, and the beauty of his Syriac verse earned him the nickname "Lyre of the Holy Spirit."

677   **Like the sun** "Just as God's creature, the sun, is one and the same the world over, so also does the Church's preaching shine everywhere to enlighten all men who want to come to a knowledge of the truth."
ST. IRENAEUS (c. 130–c. 202), ASIA MINOR (TURKEY)/FRANCE

678 **Seeing God in everything**

"Give me a heart to find out thee,
And read thee everywhere."
JOHN KEBLE (1792–1866), ENGLAND

679 **SCRIPTURAL INSPIRATION**
Scholars tend to agree that the Bible was
written, edited, and compiled by human
beings under inspiration from God. Benjamin
Warfield (1851–1921) claims it is "in every part
expressive of his mind" and that the various
human authors, such as Paul, were "prepared"
for their duties by God, who revealed as much
as was necessary for their task to be successful.

680 **Follow the divine** "I have often noticed how gladly he [St.
Francis of Sales] left the Holy Spirit to do his work freely in souls
… and guided them as they were led by God, leaving them to
follow the divine inspirations, rather than his own instructions."
JEANNE FRANÇOISE DE CHANTAL (1572–1641), FRANCE

681 **Preaching of the apostles** "How could twelve uneducated men, who lived on lakes and rivers and deserts, conceive of such a great enterprise? Their preaching was clearly divinely inspired."
ST. JOHN CHRYSOSTOM (c. 347–407), ASIA MINOR (TURKEY)

682 **Good use** "Employ whatever God has entrusted you with, in doing good ... in every possible kind and degree."
JOHN WESLEY (1703–1791), ENGLAND

683 **In heaven and on earth** "Yours, O Lord, are the greatness, the power, the glory, the victory, and the majesty: for all that is in the heavens and on the earth is yours ... and you art exalted as head above all."
1 CHRONICLES 29:11

---

684 **GUIDED BY THE SPIRIT**
According to the apostle Paul, Christ's followers should be inspired and informed in their lives by the Holy Spirit, not by the "desires of the flesh. For what the flesh desires is opposed

to the Spirit, and what the Spirit desires is opposed to the flesh." Whereas the "works of the flesh" include "strife, jealousy, anger ... the fruit of the Spirit is love, joy, peace, patience, kindness, generosity, faithfulness, gentleness, and self-control" (Galatians 5:16–25).

---

685 **Refuge** "The name of the Lord is a strong tower; the righteous run to it and are safe."
PROVERBS 18:10

686 **Lighten my darkness** St. Francis of Assisi (c. 1182–1226) made it his mission to take Christ's gospel out of the cloister and into the world of the poor and frail. He prayed for inspiration and guidance from the Holy Spirit, to "enlighten the darkness of my heart." He wished to be given "a correct faith, a certain hope" that he might better be able to "carry out your ... true command."

687 **Effortless beauty** Many Christians have seen in the beauty of nature the hand of its divine maker: "Consider the lilies, how they

grow; they neither toil nor spin; yet I tell you, even Solomon in all his glory was not clothed like one of these" (Luke 12:27).

688   The Flower

"How fresh, O Lord, how sweet and clean
Are Thy returns! even as the flowers in Spring,
To which, besides their own demean,
The late-past frost tributes of pleasure bring,
Grief melts away

Like snow in May,
As if there was no such cold thing."
GEORGE HERBERT (1593–1633), ENGLAND

689 **Communication by angels** "Since God often sends his inspirations by means of his angels, we should frequently return our aspirations to him by means of the same messengers."
ST. FRANCIS OF SALES (1567–1622), FRANCE

690 **The dawn of understanding** "As he sat, the eyes of his understanding began to open. He beheld no vision, but he saw and understood many things, spiritual as well as those concerning faith and learning. This took place with so great an illumination that these things appeared to be something altogether new."
ST. IGNATIUS OF LOYOLA (1491–1556), SPAIN

691 **Raise your eyes** "I will lift up mine eyes unto the hills, from where will my help come?"
PSALM 121:1

DOUBT

692   **Human nature** To imagine life without ever doubting, would be to deny an intrinsic element of human psychology. The American mystic Thomas Merton (1915–1968) observed that, **"Underlying all life is the ground of doubt" (693)**, while Miguel de Unamuno (1864–1936) went further in claiming that **"a faith that does not doubt is a dead faith" (694)**.

695   **Wrestling with faith**
"Faith, without trouble or fighting, is a suspicious faith; for true faith is a fighting, wrestling faith."
RALPH ERSKINE (1685–1752), SCOTLAND

696   **Walking on water** Venturing into the unknown can be daunting, and when the going gets tough, our resolve is tested. So it was when Peter ventured onto Lake Galilee (Matthew 14:22–33). Following Jesus' example, he began walking on the water. But a gust of wind caused him to doubt his ability, and he started to sink. Peter's experience reminds us that doubt in times of crisis betrays a lack of trust in God's care. As Jesus said, "Take heart ... do not be afraid!" God will support you.

697 DOUBTING THOMAS

In John's gospel (14:5–6), Thomas the apostle asks Jesus, "we do not know where you are going; how can we know the way?" To which Jesus gives his famous, enigmatic reply: "I am the way, and the truth, and the life. No one comes to the Father except through me." Later, following reports that Jesus had risen from the dead, Thomas needed to touch Christ's wounds in order to believe in the Resurrection. But once convinced, he was the first to declare the divinity of Jesus: "My Lord and my God!" (John 20:28).

698 **Strength from doubt** "The disbelief of Thomas has done more for our faith than the faith of the other disciples. As he touches Christ and is won over to belief, every doubt is cast aside and our faith is strengthened."
POPE ST. GREGORY I, THE GREAT (c. 540–604), ITALY

699 **Finding meaning** "The life of faith is a continually renewed victory over doubt, a continually renewed grasp of meaning in the midst of meaninglessness."
LESSLIE NEWBIGIN (1909–1998), ENGLAND

700 **For good or ill** St. Clare of Assisi (c. 1194–1253), a friend of St. Francis and founder of the Poor Clares order, suffered from ill health, but regarded her condition with equanimity: "Gladly endure whatever goes against you," she maintained, and "do not let good fortune lift you up: for these things destroy faith." Doubt can invade the mind as much with good fortune as with bad.

701 **Honest Habakkuk** The Old Testament prophet Habakkuk asked why, if God is all-powerful, does he tolerate sin (Habakkuk 1).

Despite these doubts, he was convinced that God's justice would prevail: "the cup in the Lord's right hand will come around" (2:16), and that those who suffered would be redeemed.

702 **Reward in time** "Faith is to believe what you do not yet see; the reward for this faith is to see what you believe."
ST. AUGUSTINE OF HIPPO (354–430), NORTH AFRICA

703 **Battles of faith** "If God promises something, then faith must fight a long and bitter fight, for reason or the flesh judges that God's promises are impossible. Therefore faith must battle against reason and its doubts."
MARTIN LUTHER (1483–1546), GERMANY

---

704 **THE TEMPTATION OF JESUS**
After a 40-day fast in the desert, famished and at his most vulnerable, Jesus was tempted, or tested, three times by Satan (Matthew 4:1–11) to see whether he would misuse his powers. His first test involved turning the desert stones

into bread—a challenge he resisted, despite his hunger. But each temptation he faced was relevant to his teaching, and helped him clarify his ministry. The way to God is not through military conquest or demonstrations of power, but through repentance and forgiveness. Many of us will face difficult decisions in times of doubt, perhaps when our reserves are low, as Jesus' were, but we must focus on doing God's will, and not on more selfish pursuits.

---

705 **Deepest fear** "... the state of having to depend solely on God is what we all dread most ... It is good of Him to force us; but dear me, how hard to feel that it is good at the time."
C.S. LEWIS (1898–1963), ENGLAND

706 **Entering tranquillity** "[H]ow great peace and quietness would he possess who should cut off all vain anxiety and place all his confidence in God."
THOMAS À KEMPIS (c. 1380–1471), GERMANY

707   **However tough** According to the cardinal John Henry Newman (1801–1890), "Ten thousand difficulties do not make one doubt."

708   **Placid calm?** A sure faith cannot expect to be free of occasional doubt or anxiety. The English reverend Charles Hodge (1797–1878) maintained that "believers have a perpetual conflict with their own diffidence, and are far from placing their consciences in a placid calm never disturbed by any storms."

709   **If in doubt**
"Trust in the Lord with all your heart …
and he will make straight your paths."
PROVERBS 3:5–6

710   **Hope in unlikely places** "Faith, like a jackal, feeds among the tombs, and even from these dead doubts she gathers her most vital hope."
HERMAN MELVILLE (1819–1891), USA

711   **Not forgotten** "Live in faith and hope, though it be in darkness,

for in this darkness God protects the soul."
ST. JOHN OF THE CROSS (1542–1591), SPAIN

712   **Be single-minded** "If any of you is lacking in wisdom, ask God, who gives to all generously and ungrudgingly, and it will be given you. But ask in faith, never doubting, for the one who doubts is like a wave of the sea, driven and tossed by the wind; for the doubter, being double-minded and unstable in every way, must not expect to receive anything from the Lord."
JAMES 1:5–8

713   **In the dark** "If a man wishes to be sure of the road he treads on, he must close his eyes and walk in the dark."
ST. JOHN OF THE CROSS (1542–1591), SPAIN

FREEDOM

714   **Freedom to choose** "There are no galley slaves in the royal vessel of divine love—every man works his oar voluntarily."
JEAN PIERRE CAMUS (1582–1652), FRANCE

715   **Of masters and slaves** "He that is kind is free, though he be a slave; he that is cruel is a slave, though he be a king."
ST. AUGUSTINE OF HIPPO (354–430), NORTH AFRICA

716   **Uncontained joy**
"He who binds to himself a joy
Does the winged life destroy;
But he who kisses the joy as it flies
Lives in eternity's sun rise."
WILLIAM BLAKE (1757–1827), ENGLAND

---

717   **FREE WILL**
Some early Christians believed that God, being all-powerful, must have control over what people do and is therefore responsible for sin. However, Paul the apostle and, later,

St. Augustine of Hippo (354–430), the great doctor of the church, established that God had deliberately granted humans free will to choose between good and evil, as had been demonstrated by Adam and Eve in the Garden of Eden. In *Free Choice of the Will*, Augustine argued that sin was not created by God, but is the misuse of our free will. This concept was also taught by the Italian church father St. Ambrose (c. 339–397), who declared that we have no "servile necessity," for we "act with free will, whether we are disposed to virtue or inclined to vice."

718 **Wish to embrace** "God, having placed good and evil in our power, has given us full freedom of choice; he does not keep back the unwilling, but embraces the willing."
ST. JOHN CHRYSOSTOM (c. 347–407), ASIA MINOR (TURKEY)

719 **Breaking the shackles** Jesus reminds his listeners that no sinner is free: "everyone who commits sin is a slave to sin." But if you follow the word of God, "you will know the truth, and the truth will set you free" (John 8:31–33).

---

720 THE EXODUS

The Exodus, or escape of the Israelites from Egypt (Exodus 12–13), is a key event in the Old Testament in which God liberates his people from oppression. For Christians, it not only points the way to spiritual freedom but proves that God will not abandon the faithful: "By faith the people passed through the Red Sea as if it were dry land" (Hebrews 11:29).

---

721 Two freedoms "There are two freedoms—the false, where a man is free to do what he likes; the true, where a man is free to do what he ought."

CHARLES KINGSLEY (1819–1875), ENGLAND

722 In God's love "God forces no one, for love cannot compel, and

God's service, therefore, is a thing of perfect freedom."
HANS DENCK (c.1495–1527), GERMANY

723   Contradiction? "A Christian man is the most free lord of all, and
subject to none; a Christian man is the most dutiful servant of all,
and subject to every one."
MARTIN LUTHER (1483–1546), GERMANY

724   Freedom in Spirit "For the law of the Spirit of life in Christ Jesus
has set you free from the law of sin and of death."
ROMANS 8:2

725   Do not abuse your freedom Since Christ's gospel is
open to all, Paul the apostle endeavored to bring together
people from different cultural backgrounds. Over the question
of eating meat that may be forbidden to some, he advised
that his church should be careful not to offend another, that
they should have consideration for "the other's conscience, not
your own." For, although "all things are lawful ... not all things
are beneficial" (1 Corinthians 10:23). We should not allow

ourselves to be compromised: "For why should my liberty be subject to the judgment of someone else's conscience" (1 Corinthians 10:29).

726   **Beyond life's grind** "There the wicked cease from troubling, and there the weary are at rest. There the prisoners are at ease together; they do not hear the voice of the taskmaster. The small and the great are there, and the slaves are free from their masters."
JOB 3:17–19

727   **True liberty** "There is no true liberty except the liberty of the happy who cleave to the eternal law."
ST. AUGUSTINE OF HIPPO (354–430), NORTH AFRICA

728   **Christian freedom and love** "For you were called to freedom, brothers and sisters; only do not use your freedom as an opportunity for self-indulgence, but through love become slaves to one another."
GALATIANS 5:13

729　**Free beings** "We are free beings and sons of God. We are called to share with God the work of creating the truth of our identity. We can evade this responsibility by playing with masks, and this pleases us because it can appear at times to be a free and creative way of living."
THOMAS MERTON (1915–1968), USA

730　**Charter of freedom** In 1215 the barons of England demanded fair treatment from their unscrupulous king, John, in accordance with the law of the land. The charter that resulted from this, the Magna Carta, was an important step toward creating a fair and free society founded on Christian principles. Its overriding dictum was: "No free man shall be taken or imprisoned or dispossessed, or outlawed or exiled, or in any way destroyed, nor will we go upon him, nor will we send against him, except by the lawful judgement of his peers or by the law of the land."

731　**Not licence** "None can love freedom heartily, but good men; the rest love not freedom, but licence."
JOHN MILTON (1608–1674), ENGLAND

732 **Loosing worldly ties** The medieval mystic Thomas à Kempis (c. 1380–1471) taught how we should seek spiritual perfection by following the example of Christ: "Who [is] more free than he who desires nothing upon earth?" Only then can a person "turn freely to the things of God." The passions and unnecessary attachments bind us to the world and block our path to God.

733 **Like a bird released**
"We have escaped like
a bird from the snare
of the fowlers;
the snare is broken,
and we have escaped."
PSALM 124:7

734 **Abolition of slavery** William Wilberforce (1759–1833) was an English social reformer whose evangelical faith inspired him to campaign for more than 20 years in Parliament for the abolition of slavery. This was finally achieved in 1807. Thereafter he continued his struggle to ensure the liberty of all slaves throughout the British Empire. The following Barbadian slave song acknowledges his efforts:

"Oh, me good friend, Mr Wilberforce, make we free!
God Almighty thank ye! God Almighty thank ye!
God Almighty, make we free!" [Barbados 1816]

735   **Within our reach** "The power of choosing good and evil is within the reach of us all."
ORIGEN OF ALEXANDRIA (c.185–254), ASIA MINOR (TURKEY)

736   **Unchained** "For freedom Christ has set us free."
GALATIANS 5:1

737   **God-given power**
"For what is freedom, but the unfettered use
Of all powers which God for use had given?"
SAMUEL TAYLOR COLERIDGE (1772–1834), ENGLAND

738   **Spiritual liberty** "The cause of freedom is the cause of God."
WILLIAM LISLE BOWLES (1762–1850), ENGLAND

Family Life

Hearth & Home   274
Procreation & Birth   282
Marriage   292
Sons & Daughters   302
Posterity   311

HEARTH & HOME

739 **From heaven** "The home came from heaven. Modeled on the Father's house and the many mansions, and meant the one to be a training place for the other, the home is one of the gifts of the Lord Jesus—a special creation of Christianity."
JAMES HAMILTON (1814–1867), ENGLAND

740 **Domestic perspective** "Let us decorate our souls rather than our houses....What will your house profit you? ... You cannot take your house with you but you will surely take your soul with you."
ST. JOHN CHRYSOSTOM (c. 347–407), ASIA MINOR (TURKEY)

741 **Welcome Jesus** "Listen! I am standing at the door, knocking; if you hear my voice and open the door, I will come in to you and eat with you, and you with me"
REVELATION 3:20

742 **God's direction**
"Unless the Lord builds the house,
   those who build it labor in vain."
PSALM 127:1

743   **Where love is**
"Better is a dinner of vegetables
    where love is
than a fatted ox and hatred
    with it."
PROVERBS 15:17

744   **Building a home** As the Bible makes clear, a home is far
more than just a building: "By wisdom a house is built, and by
understanding it is established; by knowledge the rooms are filled
with all precious and pleasant riches" (Proverbs 24:3–4).

745   **Light in a dark place** "[A] home … may be a light shining in a
dark place, a silent witness to the reality and the love of God."
OLIVE WYON (1881–1996), ENGLAND

746   **Loving care** "Happiness is to be found only in the home where
God is loved and honored, where each one loves, and helps, and
cares for the others."
THÉOPHANE VÉNARD (1829–1861), FRANCE

747   **Spiritual gel** "A family that prays together stays together."
MOTHER TERESA (1910–1997), INDIA

748   **A humble hearth** "The ties that bind the wealthy and the proud to home may be forged on earth, but those which link the poor man to his humble hearth ... bear the stamp of heaven."
CHARLES DICKENS (1812–1870), ENGLAND

749   **Boundaries** "The Jordan looms as a decisive boundary in the Bible ... laden with symbolic power. It is the boundary between the precariousness of the wilderness and the confidence of at-home-ness."
WALTER BRUEGGEMANN (BORN 1933), GERMANY

---

750   **FACING LIFE'S STORMS**
In Matthew (7:24–27), Jesus uses the parable of houses built on different foundations to suggest how we can stand firm in the face of life's storms: a house built on sand will be washed away in a storm, while one that rests

on rock is unshakable. So it is in trying times—
those whose faith is shallow will flounder, while
those whose faith is strong will survive.

---

751   The church as home?
"Home is the place where, when you have to go there,
They have to take you in ...
Something you somehow haven't to deserve."
ROBERT LEE FROST (1874–1963), USA

752   Happy home "I will have no sadness in my house."
ST. PHILIP NERI (1515–1595), ITALY

753   Be not wild "Like a bird that strays from its nest is one who
strays from home."
PROVERBS 27:8

754   Homeless The Catholic priest and writer Henri Nouwen
(1932–1996) encapsulates the tragedy of homelessness:
"Probably no word better summarizes the suffering of our times

than the word 'homeless'. It reveals one of our ... most painful conditions, the condition of not having a sense of belonging, of not having a place where we can feel safe, cared for, protected, and loved."

755 **In peace** "As you enter the house, greet it. If the house is worthy, let your peace come upon it."
MATTHEW 10:12

756 **Spiritual home**
"You who live in the shelter of the
  Most High [the Almighty] ...
will say to the Lord, 'My refuge
  and my fortress;
my God, in whom I trust.'"
PSALM 91:1–2

757 **Strangers** "Do not neglect to show hospitality to strangers, for by doing that some have entertained angels without knowing it."
HEBREWS 13:2

758 **A consecrated house** "Now my [the Lord's] eyes will be open and my ears attentive to the prayer that is made in this place. For now I have chosen and consecrated this house so that my name may be there forever; my eyes and heart will be there for ever."
2 CHRONICLES 7:15

759 **Avoid laziness**
"She looks well to the ways
    of her household,
and does not eat the bread
    of idleness."
PROVERBS 31:27

760 **A refuge** "[H]ome ... is the
... shelter, not only from
injury, but from all terror,
doubt and division."
JOHN RUSKIN (1819–1900),
ENGLAND

761   **Honor to all visitors** "Let all guests that come be received like Christ, for he will say, 'I was a stranger and ye took me in' (Matthew 25:35)."
ST. BENEDICT OF NURSIA (c. 480–c. 547), ITALY

762   **Inviolable home** "Remember the rights of the savage, as we call him. Remember that the happiness of his humble home, remember that the sanctity of life in the hill villages of Afghanistan, among the winter snows, is as inviolable in the eye of the Almighty God as can be your own."
WILLIAM EWART GLADSTONE (1809–1898), ENGLAND

763   **Loving yet practical** "To give our Lord a perfect hospitality, Mary and Martha [Luke 10:38–41] must combine."
ST. TERESA OF AVILA (1515–1582), SPAIN

764   **Growing away** For the Anglican poet T.S. Eliot (1888–1965), home is: "... where one starts from. As we grow older
The world becomes stranger, the pattern more complicated
Of dead and living."

765 **God's forest home** "I am the heat of your hearth on the cold winter nights, the friendly shade screening you from the summer sun.... I am the beam that holds your house, the board of your table, the bed on which you lie.... You who pass by, listen to my prayer: harm me not."
PRAYER FROM PORTUGAL

766 **God's garden**
"The kiss of the sun for pardon,
The song of the birds for mirth,
One is nearer God's Heart in a garden
Than anywhere else on earth."
DOROTHY FRANCES GURNEY (1858–1932), ENGLAND

767 **God's house** The church is believed to be God's earthly abode. As Jesus declares, "My house shall be called a house of prayer" (Matthew 21:13).

768 **Stand together** "No house divided against itself will stand."
MATTHEW 12:25.

PROCREATION & BIRTH

769   **Divine command** "Be fruitful and multiply, and fill the earth."
GENESIS 1:28

770   **Life** "Is it that the passion shown in the birth of a child gives
us a glimpse into the passion of God giving birth to creation?"
CHOAN-SENG SONG (BORN 1929), TAIWAN

771   **Announcement of Christ** "For a child has been born for us,
a son given to us."
ISAIAH 9:6

772   **Mystery of creation** For many Christian writers, the miracle of
creation is expressed in the breathtaking appearance of new life:
"Baby:
Unwritten history!
Unfathomed mystery!"
JOSIAH GILBERT HOLLAND (1819–1881), USA

773   **Every birth is holy**
"By God's birth

All common birth is holy; birth
Is all at Christmas time, and wholly blest."
ANNE RIDLER (1912–2001), ENGLAND

774 **Sacred word of God**
"Before I formed you in the
womb I knew you,
and before you were born I
consecrated you;
I appointed you a prophet to the nations."
JEREMIAH 1:5

775 **God in all** "God is eternally pregnant."
MEISTER ECKHART (1260–1327), GERMANY

776 **Pain into joy** "When a woman is in labor, she has pain, because
her hour has come. But when her child is born, she no longer
remembers the anguish because of the joy of having brought a
human being into the world."
JOHN 16:21

777   **Immaculate conception** Roman Catholics believe that the Virgin Mary, unlike the rest of humanity, was "kept free from all stain of original sin," as Pope Pius IX (1846–1878) declared.

778   **Miraculous** "All teaching about Mary the Mother of God points us to the uniqueness of Jesus Christ. The miracle of his birth shows us that he is God-with-us ... we are adopted as children of the Father in the Holy Spirit. We look to Mary as a Mother."
CORMAC MURPHY-O'CONNOR (BORN 1932), ENGLAND

779   **Origin divine**
"Our birth is but a sleep and a forgetting.
The Soul that rises with us, our life's Star,
Hath had elsewhere its setting,
And cometh from afar;
Not in entire forgetfulness,
And not in utter nakedness,
But trailing clouds of glory do we come
From God, who is our home."
WILLIAM WORDSWORTH (1770–1850), ENGLAND

780 **Mother of all** "The man named his wife Eve, because she was the mother of all living."
GENESIS 3:20

781 **Precious and unblemished** "Children are living jewels, dropped unstained from heaven."
ROBERT POLLOCK (1798–1827), SCOTLAND

782 **Utter beauty** "The beauty that I saw in Our Lady was extraordinary, although I didn't make out any particular details except the form of her face in general and that her garment was of the most brilliant white, not dazzling, but soft. Our Lady seemed to me to be a very young girl."
ST. TERESA OF AVILA (1515–1582), SPAIN

783 **Greatness in a tiny womb** "Cling to His most sweet Mother who carried a son Whom the heavens could not contain; and yet she carried Him in the little enclosure of her holy womb and held him on her virginal lap."
ST. CLARE OF ASSISI (c. 1194–1253), ITALY

784   **No life without God**

"Upon you I have leaned from my birth;
it was you who took me from my mother's womb.
My praise is continually of you."

PSALM 71:6

785   **We bring nothing** "We brought nothing into the world, so that
we can take nothing out of it."

1 TIMOTHY 6:7

786   **Stranger than fiction** "The Incarnation is the most delightful,
human, visually beautiful and delicate of all Christian beliefs. The
idea of God's son coming to earth in a manger, is beyond the
power of any mortal imagination to invent and is so obviously
true that anyone who denies it must have the feelings of a brute."

PAUL JOHNSON (BORN 1928), ENGLAND

787   **How?** "Mary said to the angel, 'How can this be, since I am a
virgin?'"

LUKE 1:34

788 CHRIST'S NATIVITY

A key element of the Christian story is the birth of God's son, Jesus, in a simple stable in Bethlehem. No glorious palace, no heralding retainers, but a vulnerable baby born the savior of the world. Commemorated every year at Christmas, this beautiful tenet of the faith is a compelling narrative rooted in an everyday event—that of new life. God's incarnation through Mary links humanity with the divine and provides an ideal of maternal and feminine power abounding with tenderness and love.

789 Unarmed combat

"This little Babe, so few days old,
Is come to rifle Satan's fold;
All hell doth at his presence quake ...
For in this weak, unarmed wise,
The gates of hell he will surprise."
ROBERT SOUTHWELL (c. 1561–1595), ENGLAND

790 **Adoration of the Magi** "... there, ahead of them, went the star that they had seen at its rising, until it stopped over the place where the child was. When they saw that the star had stopped, they were overwhelmed with joy. On entering the house, they saw the child with Mary his mother; and they knelt down and paid him homage."
MATTHEW 2:9–11

791 **Breath of life** "[God] breathed into his nostrils the breath of life; and man became a living being."
GENESIS 2:7

792 **Baptism and new life** Baptism, which involves symbolic purification with water, is an important Christian sacrament that marks the beginning of a new life and a sharing in the life of Christ. In the words of Jesus, "Very truly, I tell you, no one can enter the kingdom of God without being born of water and the Spirit" (John 3:5).

793 **All things bound together** "When the church baptizes a child,

that action concerns me, for that child is thereby connected to
that which is my head too, and ingrafted into that body whereof
I am a member."
JOHN DONNE (1572–1631), ENGLAND

794   Humanity

"I also am mortal, like everyone else,
a descendant of the first-formed
    child of earth;
and in the womb of a mother I was
    molded into flesh,
within the period of ten months,
    compacted with blood,
from the seed of a man and the
    pleasure of a marriage.
And when I was born I began to
    breathe the common air,
and fell from the kindred earth;
my first sound was a cry, as is true of all."
THE WISDOM OF SOLOMON 7:1–3

MARRIAGE

795   **With this ring** "With this Ring I thee wed, with
my body I thee worship, and with all my worldly
goods I thee endow."
BOOK OF COMMON PRAYER (1662), ENGLAND

796   **One flesh** "Therefore a man leaves his father and mother and
clings to his wife, and they become one flesh."
GENESIS 2:24

797   **Lovely sight**
"I take pleasure in three things,
and they are beautiful in the
sight of God and of
mortals:
agreement among brothers and
sisters, friendship among
neighbors,
and a wife and a husband who
live in harmony."
ECCLESIASTICUS 25:1

798   **Pleasure** "Enjoy life with the wife whom you love, all the days of your vain life that are given you under the sun, because that is your portion in life."
ECCLESIASTES 9:9

799   **Undefiled** "Let marriage be held in honor by all, and let the marriage bed be kept undefiled."
HEBREWS 13:4

800   **Labor of love** Genesis 29 tells how the patriarch Jacob fell in love with Rachel, daughter of the mean farmer Laban. Jacob labored seven years for Laban to win Rachel's hand in marriage. But Laban tricked Jacob by substituting Rachel's elder sister Leah at the wedding and then made Jacob promise another seven years' labor for Rachel's hand. Between them, Leah and Rachel bore the twelve sons who became ancestors of the tribes of Israel.

801   **Uncertain affair** A married couple's life together is an adventure, and only time will tell whether husband or wife is good: "A prudent wife is from the Lord" (Proverbs 19:14).

802 **Marriage ceremony** "[W]e are gathered together here
in the sight of God ... to join together this Man and this
Woman in holy Matrimony; which is an honorable estate,
instituted of God in the time of man's innocency, signifying
unto us the mystical union that is betwixt Christ and his Church
... and therefore is not by any to be enterprised ... unadvisedly,
lightly, or wantonly, to satisfy men's carnal lusts and appetites ...
but reverently, discreetly, advisedly, soberly, and ...
duly considering the causes for which Matrimony
was ordained."
BOOK OF COMMON PRAYER (1662), ENGLAND

803 **Bond between equals**
"My beloved is mine and I am his,
he pastures his flock among the lilies.
Until the day breathes
and the shadows flee,
turn, my beloved, be like a gazelle,
or a young stag on the cleft mountains."
SONG OF SOLOMON 2:16–17

804   **Before you leap** "Since marriage is designed by Providence as a life, the worst possible way of embarking upon that life is by the premature exercise of what is meant to be its final consummation."

HUBERT VAN ZELLER (1905–1984), ENGLAND

---

805   **MARRIAGE GUIDANCE**
St. Paul advised that those who are able to, should abstain from marriage, as he did (unusually for his time), but those who cannot, should marry (1 Corinthians 7:1–7). In allowing this "concession," Paul is really warning against licentiousness: "It is better to marry than to be aflame with passion." But whether single or married, he says, Christians should always put God first.

---

806   **Conjugal rights** "The husband should give to his wife her conjugal rights, and likewise the wife to her husband. For the wife does not have authority over her own body, but the husband

does; likewise the husband does not have authority over his own body, but the wife does."
1 CORINTHIANS 7:3–4

807 **Good thing** "He who finds a wife finds a good thing, and obtains favor from the Lord."
PROVERBS 18:22

808 **Stay together** "Therefore what God has joined together, let no one separate."
MATTHEW 19:6

809 **Christ's bride** Many Christians view the institution of marriage as comparable to the relationship between the church and Christ, with the sacrament of marriage as a symbol of Christ's love for his church: "Husbands, love your wives just as Christ loved the church" (Ephesians 5:25).

810 **Forever** "[T]he day of a believer's death is his marriage day, the day of his fullest enjoyment of Christ. No husband can say to his wife, what Christ says to the believer, "I will never leave you, nor forsake you."

JOHN FLAVEL (1627–1691), ENGLAND

811   **A balm** "Marriage was ordained for a remedy and to increase the world and for the man to help the woman and the woman the man, with all love and kindness."

WILLIAM TYNDALE (c. 1494–1536), ENGLAND

812   **The greatest relationship** "There is no more lovely, friendly or charming relationship, communion or company, than a good marriage."

MARTIN LUTHER (1483–1546), GERMANY

813   **Hymn to marriage**
"O perfect Love, all human thought transcending,
Lowly we kneel in prayer before Thy throne,
That theirs may be the love which knows no ending
Whom Thou for evermore dost join in one."

DOROTHY FRANCES GURNEY (1858–1932), ENGLAND

814 THE WEDDING AT CANA

Jesus' first miracle (John 2) was performed at a wedding in Galilee. Alerted to the short supply of wine, he instructed the guests to bring him jars filled with water. They obliged, and when the jars were tipped up they found the water had turned into wine. The old Jewish dispensation is transformed through the work of the Lord into the new fine wine of the Gospel.

815   First love yourself "He who loves his wife loves himself."
EPHESIANS 5:28

816   Heaven's most precious gift to man "A good wife is
heaven's last best gift to man; his angel and minister of graces
innumerable; his gem of many virtues; his casket of jewels; her
voice his sweet music; her smiles his brightest day; her kiss the
guardian of his innocence; her arms the pale of his safety the
balm of his health, the balsam of his life; her industry, his
surest wealth; her economy, his safest steward; her lips, his
faithful counselors; her bosom, the softest pillow of his cares;
and her prayers, the ablest advocates of heaven's blessings on
his head."
JEREMY TAYLOR (1613–1667), ENGLAND

817   In unison
"O magnify the Lord with me
and let us exalt his name
together."
PSALM 34:3

818   **Spiritual partnership** "The unbelieving husband is made holy through his wife, and the unbelieving wife is made holy through her husband."

1 CORINTHIANS 7:14

819   **The unbeliever** "If any believer has a wife who is an unbeliever, and she consents to live with him, he should not divorce her. And if any woman has a husband who is an unbeliever, and he consents to live with her, she should not divorce him. For the unbelieving husband is made holy through his wife, and the unbelieving wife is made holy through her husband."

1 CORINTHIANS 7:12-14

820   **Help one another** "Watch over the hearts and lives of one another, judging the condition of each other's souls, and the strength or weakness of each other's sins and graces, and the failings of each others lives, so that you may be able to apply to one another the most suitable help."

RICHARD BAXTER (1615–1691), ENGLAND

SONS & DAUGHTERS

821 **Cherish your children** "Acceptance and appreciation tell the child that he or she is of tremendous worth. And I can only express my acceptance and appreciation through being affectionate—and available."
JOSH McDOWELL (BORN 1939), USA

822 **Cherish your parents** "Honour your parents both in your thoughts, and speech, and behaviour. Think not dishonourably ... of them in your hearts ... though you cannot honour them as rich, or wise, or godly, you must honour them as your parents."
RICHARD BAXTER (1615–1691), ENGLAND

---

823 **UNCONDITIONAL FORGIVENESS: A PRODIGAL SON**
One of the Bible's most famous parables is that of the prodigal son (Luke 15), who takes his inheritance before his father's death. When the son returns home—impoverished, having squandered the money on a life of dissipation—his father is overjoyed. He embraces and kisses him, giving orders for a

celebration to be prepared. The elder son (who all the while had been "working like a slave" for his father) protests, but the father replies that they had to celebrate the return of one who "was dead and has come to life." Such is the power of parental love and forgiveness.

---

824 **Let go** "You may give them [your sons and daughters] your love but not your thoughts. For they have their own thoughts. You may house their bodies but not their souls. For their souls dwell in the house of tomorrow, which you cannot visit, even in your dreams."
KAHLIL GIBRAN (1883–1931), LEBANON/USA

825 **Family honor** "Ask yourselves, each of you, Have I been a good
brother? ...son? ...husband? ...father? ...servant? If not,
all professions of religion will avail me nothing."
CHARLES KINGSLEY (1819–1875), ENGLAND

826 **The first homicide** Fraternal strife results in tragedy when, as
Genesis 4 relates, Adam's and Eve's firstborn son, Cain, murders

his shepherd brother, Abel, out of jealousy. Division arose because "the Lord had regard for Abel and his offering, but for Cain and his offering he had no regard" (4:5). Thus, "Cain rose up against his brother Abel, and killed him" (4:8).

---

827 SIBLING RIVALRY: JOSEPH AND HIS BROTHERS
Genesis tells of how Joseph was spoiled by his parents, Jacob and Rachel. His brothers resented this favoritism and when their father gave Joseph a "long robe with sleeves" (Genesis 37), their jealousy increased. They threw Joseph into a well (telling their father he had died) and later sold him into slavery. But Joseph rose to a position of power in his adopted country of Egypt and was able to help his brothers, who one day came begging. With fortunes now reversed, the brothers forgot their grievances and discovered their familial love. Joseph, whose gift for interpreting dreams won him political status, saw the entire episode as divinely ordained. Insisting

his brothers should not feel guilty for their crimes, he explained "it was not you who sent me here, but God" (Genesis 45:8).

---

828 **Change of heart** Adopting the spirit of Jesus' gospel of love brings a new attitude to family members. As the Old Testament prophet Malachi foretold, "He will turn the hearts of parents to their children and the hearts of children to their parents" (4:6).

829 **Of heaven** "Let the little children come to me ... for it is to such as these that the kingdom of heaven belongs."
MATTHEW 19:14

830 **Nurture** "And, fathers, do not provoke your children to anger, but bring them up in the discipline and instruction of the Lord."
EPHESIANS 6:4

831 **Value of discipline** "A wise child loves discipline, but a scoffer does not listen to rebuke."
PROVERBS 13:1

832   **Love behind the reprimand**
"My child, do not despise the
Lord's discipline ...
For the Lord reproves the one he loves,
as a father the son in whom he delights."
PROVERBS 3:11–12

833   **Right upbringing** "Train children in the right way, and when
old, they will not stray."
PROVERBS 22:6

834   **A quiver full** "Lo, children are an heritage of the Lord: and the
fruit of the womb is his reward. As arrows are in the hand of a
mighty man; so are children of the youth. Happy is the man that
hath a quiver full of them."
PSALM 127:3–5 [KJV]

835   **Glorious grandchildren** "Grandchildren are the crown of the
aged, and the glory of children is their parents."
PROVERBS 17:6

836 **Live long** "Children, obey your parents in the Lord, for this is right. 'Honor your father and mother'—this is the first commandment with a promise: 'so that it may be well with you and you may live long on the earth.'"
EPHESIANS 6:1–3

---

837 **THE DAUGHTER OF JAIRUS**
The story of Jairus, whose daughter was mortally sick (Mark 5:21–43), shows the power of faith that comes from a father's deep love for his daughter. Jairus's faith is such that he has no doubt that when Jesus lays his hands on the girl she will be healed. Even when others claim she is dead, he does not lose heart, since Jesus has assured him she is "sleeping." And sure enough, after Jesus utters "Little girl, get up" (Mark 5:41), the child is cured.

---

838 **Formative years** The early years of a child's development are crucial in determining their nature and personality in later life.

One of the first Jesuits, St. Francis Xavier, is credited with the famous saying, "Give me a child until he is seven and I will give you the man."
ST. FRANCIS XAVIER (1506–1552), SPAIN

839   **God's family** Baptized members of the church are considered God's adopted sons and daughters: "I will welcome you, and I will be your father, and you shall be my sons and daughters, says the Lord Almighty" (2 Corinthians 6:18).

840   **As God loves us** "Remember that God loves your soul, not in some aloof, impersonal way, but passionately, with the adoring, cherishing love of a parent for a child."
HENRI DE TOURVILLE (1842–1903), FRANCE

841   **By their actions**
"Even children make themselves
    known by their acts,
by whether what they do is pure and right."
PROVERBS 20:11

[309]

842 **Sympathetic ear** "Jesus was the first great teacher of men who showed a genuine sympathy for childhood."
EDWARD EGGLESTON (1837–1902), USA

843 **Unforced religion** "Never force religious instruction on your child. It is far more important for him to feel the impact of your faith ... your children will sense it in your daily life and in your contact with them."
JOHANN CHRISTOPH ARNOLD (BORN 1940), GERMANY

844 **Out of harm's way** "Precious Savior! come in spirit, and lay Thy strong, gentle grasp of love on our dear boys and girls, and keep these our lambs from the fangs of the wolf."
THEODORE LEDYARD CUYLER (1822–1909), USA

POSTERITY

845   **Future peoples** According to the Bible, the peopling of the world is a blessing from God that was first given to Noah and his sons. As sole survivors of the Flood, their families will turn into "nations spread abroad on the earth" (Genesis 10:32).

846   **Promise of offspring to Jacob** "And the Lord stood beside him and said, I am the Lord, the God of Abraham your father and the God of Isaac; the land on which you lie I will give to you and your offspring; and your offspring shall be like the dust of the earth, and you shall spread abroad to the west and to the east and to the north and to the south; and all the families of the earth shall be blessed in you and in your offspring."
GENESIS 28:13–14

847   **Great nation** "I will make of you a great nation, and I will bless you, and make your name great, so that you will be a blessing."
GENESIS 12:2

848   **With hindsight** "Posterity will some day laugh at the foolishness of modern materialistic philosophy. The more

I study nature, the more I am amazed at the Creator."
LOUIS PASTEUR (1822–1895), FRANCE

849 **Stars in the sky** "The angel of the Lord called to Abraham …
and said … I will make your offspring as numerous as the stars of
heaven and as the sand that is on the seashore."
GENESIS 22:15–17

---

850 **THE NEW COVENANT**
The Old Testament covenant between God
and his chosen people was a pledge of
obedience to the Commandments given to
Moses at Mount Sinai. But the Israelites proved
disloyal by breaking these laws. The prophet
Jeremiah looked forward to the day when a
new covenant would be written on people's

inheritance" (Hebrews 9:15). Thus the ancient promise made to Abraham that "all peoples on earth will be blessed" (Genesis 12:3) is fulfilled in Christ.

---

851 **Preserving the environment** It is a Christian duty to look after our planet. God entrusted humankind "to till and keep" the garden of Eden (Genesis 2:15). This command extends to stewardship of the Earth—the world was created for all to enjoy, but it is within humankind's power to destroy it or to preserve it for posterity.

852 **Look to the future** The French scientist, philosopher, and theologian Blaise Pascal (1623–1662) was clear about what humanity's focus should be: "The present is never our goal: the past and present are our means: the future alone is our goal."

854   **Unknowing** "God will not suffer man to have the knowledge of things to come; for if he had prescience of his prosperity, he would be careless; and, understanding of his adversity, he would be senseless."
ST. AUGUSTINE OF HIPPO (354–430), NORTH AFRICA

855   **Pilgrims of hope** "Jesus said to him, 'If you wish to be perfect, go, sell your possessions, and give the money to the poor and you will have the treasure in heaven; then come follow me.'"
MATTHEW 19:21

856   **New spiritual reality** Some Christians believe the universe is slowly progressing to a point of fulfillment when all things will be gathered up in God. The French scientist and Jesuit Teilhard de Chardin (1881–1955) identified critical thresholds in an evolutionary process that puts responsibility for spiritual development in the hands of humans. A "new earth is gathering, isolating and purifying itself." He likens humanity to "leaves and flowers of a great tree, on which each appears at its time and place, according to the demands of the All."

Friends
& Neighbors

Friendship 318

Neighborhood 326

Working Together 339

Travel 350

Peace 361

FRIENDSHIP

857   **Be concerned** Friendships are precious and should be nurtured. As the author of the letter to the Hebrews suggests, "Consider how to provoke one another to love and good deeds" (Hebrews 10:24). Here the word "provoke" is used in a positive sense, to encourage.

858   **Make an effort** Stimulate friendship, the Bible advises, by "not neglecting to meet together, as is the habit of some" (Hebrews 10:25).

859   **Spiritual communion** "The deepest level of communication is not communication, but communion. It is wordless. It is beyond words, and it is beyond speech, and it is beyond concept."
THOMAS MERTON (1915–1968), USA

860   **The inner spirit** "In everyone's life, at some time, our inner fire goes out. It is then burst into flame by an encounter with another human being. We should all be thankful for those people who rekindle the inner spirit."
ALBERT SCHWEITZER (1875–1965), GERMANY

861   **True value** The Christian poet, Kahlil Gibran (1883–1931), considered friendship a "sweet responsibility," to be cherished, not taken for granted, and never to be used for personal gain.

862   **No island** Over 400 years ago, in *Meditation XVII*, the great priest and poet John Donne (c. 1573–1631) reminded us of the essential inerconnectedness, the inseparable link between all humankind: "No Man is an Island, entire of itself; every man is a piece of the Continent, a part of the main."

863   **THE GREATEST COMMANDMENT**
At one point during his ministry, Jesus encapsulated the entire gospel thus: "This is my commandment, That ye love one another, as I have loved you." Jesus' love for his disciples is greater than any love, as demonstrated by the fact that he gave his life for them: "Greater love hath no man than this, that a man lay down his life for his friends" (John 15:12–15 [KJV]).

864 **Tell of your needs** "And each one should confidently make known his needs to the other, so that he might find what he needs and minister to him. And each one should love and care for his brother in all those things in which God will give him grace, as a mother loves and cares for her son."
ST. FRANCIS OF ASSISI (c. 1182–1226), ITALY

865 **Courtesy** "He who sows courtesy reaps friendship."
ST. BASIL OF CAESAREA (c. 330–c. 379), ASIA MINOR (TURKEY)

866 **Thicker than blood** "A true friend sticks closer than one's nearest kin."
PROVERBS 18:24

867 **Fellowship** "God has taught in the Scriptures the lesson of a universal brotherhood, and man must not gainsay the teaching. Shivering in the ice-bound or scorching in the tropical regions; in the

lap of luxury or in the wild hardihood of the primeval forest;
… gathering all the decencies around him like a garment,
or battling in fierce raid of crime against a world which has
disowned him, there is an inner humanness which binds me
to that man by a primitive and indissoluble bond … He is my
brother, and I cannot release myself from the obligation to do
him good."
WILLIAM MORLEY PUNSHON (1824–1881), ENGLAND

868   **A sturdy shelter**
"Faithful friends are a sturdy shelter:
Whoever finds one has found a
    treasure."
ECCLESIASTICUS 6:14

869   **Honesty** "One who gives an honest answer gives a kiss on
the lips."
PROVERBS 24:26

870   **A friend's rebuke** However hurtful at the time, a friend's frank

criticism, which is "well meant" (Proverbs 27:6), is better than **misguided friendship that "flatters with the tongue" (871)** (Proverbs 28: 23) and turns a blind eye to one's faults.

872   **Nature and religion** "Nature teaches us to love our friends, but religion our enemies."
THOMAS FULLER (1608–1661), ENGLAND

873   **Cruel to be kind**
"Faithful [are] the wounds of a friend,
But the kisses of an enemy [are] deceitful."
PROVERBS 27:6 [KJV]

874   **God as our friend** "If we address [God] as children, it is because he tells us he is our father. If we unbosom ourselves to him as a friend, it is because he calls us friends."
WILLIAM COWPER (1731–1800), ENGLAND

875   **Letter-writing** "My dear son, when you receive a letter from a friend, you should not hesitate to embrace it as a friend. It is a

great consolation for friends who are apart, that a letter can be embraced in the absence of its beloved writer."
ST. ISIDORE OF SEVILLE (c. 560–636), SPAIN

876   **Sisterhood** The famous poem *Goblin Market* by the English poet and devotional writer Christina Rossetti (1830–1894) offers a perspective on friendship that plays on the various meanings of the word "sister" (female sibling, member of a church, female friend):

"For there is no friend like a sister
In calm or stormy weather;
To cheer one on the tedious way,
To fetch one if one goes astray,
To lift one if one totters down,
To strengthen whilst one stands."

877   **Pray for each other** When we know we have done wrong, especially when we have wounded a friend, the apostle James advises, "confess your sins to one another, and pray for one another, so that you may be healed" (James 5:16).

878 Old friends
"Do not abandon old friends;
for new ones cannot equal them.
A new friend is like new wine;
when it has aged, you can drink
it with pleasure."
ECCLESIASTICUS 9:10

879 Share all food One of the first rules of the earliest Christian monasteries in Egypt was to share what we have, and ensure all are served: "And no one shall eat at all anything from field or orchard on his own before it has been served to all the brothers like."
PACHOMIUS (c. 290–346), EGYPT

880 Medicine "No medicine is more valuable, none more efficacious, none better suited to the cure of all our temporal ills than a friend to who we may turn for consolation in time of trouble— and with whom we may share our happiness in time of joy."
ST. AELRED OF RIEVAULX (c. 1109–c. 1167), ENGLAND

881 **Undying friendship** William Penn (1644–1718), a pioneer of the Society of Friends (Quakers), believed that friendship continues beyond death. "This is the comfort of Friends, that though they may be said to Die, yet their Friendship and Society are, in the best sense, ever present because *immortal*."

882 **Straight talking** "The better friends you are, the straighter you can talk, but while you are only on nodding terms, be slow to scold."
ST. FRANCIS XAVIER (1506–1552), SPAIN

NEIGHBORHOOD

883   **Pure love** "He alone loves the Creator perfectly who manifests a pure love for his neighbor."
ST. BEDE THE VENERABLE (c. 673–735), ENGLAND

884   **Everyone** The theologian St. Augustine of Hippo (354–430) taught that "neighbor" must be taken to mean every human being, just as in the Old Testament the word referred to any fellow Israelite, not just the person living next door.

885   **Love one another** "Owe no one anything, except to love one another; for the one who loves another has fulfilled the law. The commandments ... are summed up in this word, 'Love your neighbor as yourself.' Love does no wrong to a neighbor."
ROMANS 13:8–10

886   **United in God's love** "The nearer we draw to God in our love for him, the more we are united together by love for our neighbor; and the greater our union with our neighbor, the greater is our union with God."
ST. DOROTHEUS OF GAZA (6th CENTURY), PALESTINE

326

887 OFFERING SUPPORT

In his epistle to the Romans (Romans 15:1–2), Paul taught that if a neighborhood is to thrive and develop, good citizens must be prepared to support those around them, "to put up with the failings of the weak." By this he meant not to judge them, but to endeavor always to

"please our neighbor" by giving them moral support, "for the good purpose of building up the neighbor."

888 **With discretion**

"... What your eyes have seen do not hastily bring into court;
for what will you do in the end,
when your neighbor puts you to shame?
Argue your case with your neighbor directly,
and do not disclose another's secret;
or else someone who hears you will bring shame upon you,
and your ill repute will have no end."
PROVERBS 25:7–10

889 **Pulling down fences** "There are three gestures, in particular, which are capable of being signs of God at work, paths of communion and ways of discovering new dimensions of ecumenism: Avoid separating the generations; Go to meet those who cannot believe; Stand alongside the exploited."
BROTHER ROGER OF TAIZÉ (1915–2005), SWITZERLAND

890   **Hospitality to strangers** "The alien who resides with you shall be to you as the citizen among you; you shall love the stranger as yourself; for you were strangers in the land of Egypt."
LEVITICUS 19:34

891   **Simple hospitality** "Christians should offer their brethren simple and unpretentious hospitality."
ST. BASIL OF CAESAREA (c. 330–c. 379), ASIA MINOR (TURKEY)

892   **Pester not** "Let your foot be seldom in your neighbor's house, otherwise the neighbor will become weary of you and hate you."
PROVERBS 25:17

893   **Sharing** "Be hospitable to one another without complaining.... serve one another with whatever gift each of you has received."
1 PETER 4:9–10

894   **Double standards** "How rarely we weigh our neighbor in the same balance in which we weigh ourselves."
THOMAS À KEMPIS (c. 1380–1471), GERMANY

895   THE GOOD SAMARITAN

Jesus was asked by a lawyer, "Who is my neighbor?" He replied by telling the parable of the Good Samaritan (Luke 10:30–37). An innocent man was robbed and left for dead on the roadside. Two men—one a priest, the other a Levite (temple official)—passed by, ignoring the dying man. But a Samaritan was "moved with pity" when he saw him; he bandaged the man's wounds and took him to an inn where he would be cared for. When Jesus asked the lawyer "Which of these three ... was a neighbor to the man?", he replied, "The one who showed him mercy." Following this example, in 1953 the Reverend Chad Varah (1911–2007) founded The Samaritans in London, England, an organization that gives help at any hour to the desperate and suicidal.

---

896   Bearing burdens Martin Luther (1483–1546) said "the Law of

Christ is the Law of love, "meaning that we must be prepared to do as Paul said and "bear one another's burdens" (Galatians 6:2). Luther implied this was no easy task: "Christians must have strong shoulders," but "If we can overlook our own shortcomings and wrong-doings, we ought to overlook the shortcomings of others."

---

897 OPEN TO ALL

One distinguishing virtue of the early church was its openness to everyone, regardless of class, gender, or ethnic background. A leading proponent of this attitude was the evangelist St. John who, though being Jewish, ignored the contempt his people often held for their neighbors, the Samaritans. The story of the Woman from Samaria, told in John's gospel (chapter 4), illustrates how prejudice and stereotyping can be overcome if our hearts are open to all whom we encounter.

---

898 Having no expectations In *Dialog*, the mystic St. Catherine of Siena (1347–1380) recorded conversations she claimed to have had with Christ. One passage speaks of her duty to love her neighbor as though she were loving Christ: "To me in person, you cannot repay the love which I require of you. I have placed you in the midst of your fellows that you may do to them what you cannot do to me, that is to say that you may love your neighbor of free grace without expecting any return from him, and what you do to him I count as done to me."

899 **Live in harmony** "May the God of steadfastness and encouragement grant you to live in harmony with one another, in accordance with Christ Jesus, so that together you may with one voice glorify the God and Father of our Lord Jesus Christ." ROMANS 15:5–6

900 **Man for all seasons** "Is it not the great end of religion, and, in particular, the glory of Christianity, to extinguish the malignant passions; to curb the violence, to control the appetites, and to smooth the asperities of man; to make us compassionate and kind, and forgiving one to another; to make us good husbands,

good fathers, good friends; and to render us active and useful in the discharge of the relative social and civil duties?"
WILLIAM WILBERFORCE (1759–1833), ENGLAND

901 **Respect and honor** The apostle Paul taught that we should have respect for each other, even those whom we may not like very much. "Let love be genuine," he said, and "outdo one another in showing honor" to all. Strive to "love one another with mutual affection."
ROMANS 12:9–10

902 **In desire alone** One of the Ten Commandments stipulates, "You shall not covet your neighbor's house … or anything that belongs to your neighbor" (Exodus 20:17). It is, then, a sin simply to desire your neighbor's possessions.

903 **Love your enemies** Jesus turns on its head the traditional maxim of loving your neighbor and hating your enemy. He says instead that you must "Love your enemies and pray for those who persecute you" (Matthew 5:43–44). For it is not enough only to "love those who love you" (5:46). You must do good to your enemies and befriend them, so that enmity disappears.

904   **No thought of reward** "Blessed is he who does good to others and desires not that others should do him good."
ST. GILES OF ASSISI (DIED c. 1262), ITALY

905   **Keep yourself to yourself** "We should have great peace if we did not busy ourselves with what others say and do."
THOMAS À KEMPIS (c.1380–1471), GERMANY

906   **Be accommodating** "Faith, like light, should always be simple, and unbending; while love, like warmth, should beam forth on every side, and bend to every necessity of our brethren."
MARTIN LUTHER (1483–1546), GERMANY

907   **As good as the Lord** "Though we do not have our Lord with us in bodily presence, we have our neighbor, who, for the ends of love and loving service, is as good as our Lord himself."
ST. TERESA OF AVILA (1515–1582), SPAIN

908   **Reproving with love** "If thy brother hath done wrong, thou shalt neither divulge it to others, nor hate him, and smother that hatred by sullen silence; nor flatter him therein, but shalt freely and in love, tell him of his fault."
JOHN WESLEY (1703–1791), ENGLAND

909   **Gossip**
"A gossip goes about telling
    secrets,
but one who is trustworthy in
    spirit keeps a confidence."
PROVERBS 11:13

910   **No slander** "You shall not go around as a slanderer among your people."
LEVITICUS 19:16

911   **Restoring self-love** The English devotional writer C.S. Lewis (1898–1963) believed that the imperative to love thy neighbor as thyself was in part Christ's "long-term policy ... to restore ...

a new kind of self-love." Lewis asserted, "When they have really learned to love their neighbours as themselves, they will be allowed to love themselves as their neighbours."

912   **Three things** "Love for our neighbor consists of three things: to desire the greater good of everyone; to do what good we can when we can; to bear, excuse and hide others' faults."
JEAN VIANNES (1786–1859), FRANCE

913   **In any situation** "Your neighbour is the man who is next to you at the moment, the man with whom any business has brought you into contact."
GEORGE MACDONALD (1824–1905), SCOTLAND

914   **Bear no grudges** "You shall not take vengeance or bear a grudge against any of your people."
LEVITICUS 19:18

915   **On behalf of others** "Lastly, we will speak also of those works which he [man] performs towards his neighbor. For man does

not live for himself alone in this mortal body, in order to work on its account, but also for all men on earth; nay, he lives only for others and not for himself.... Thus it is impossible that he should take his ease in this life, and not work for the good of his neighbors."
MARTIN LUTHER (1483–1546), GERMANY

916 **A unifying force** "The source of hospitality is the heart of God who yearns to unite every creature within one embrace."
SOCIETY OF ST. JOHN
THE EVANGELIST

WORKING TOGETHER

917   **Mutual support** "Two are better than one, because they have a good reward for their toil. For if they fall, one will lift up the other; but woe to one who is alone and falls and does not have another to help."

ECCLESIASTES 4:9–10

918   **Building bridges** The French monk and founder of the Cistercian Order of monasteries, St. Bernard of Clairvaux (1091–1153), was a deeply religious man. But his uncompromising stance on matters of principle sometimes made him a difficult person to work with. However, he himself saw no disadvantage in such a trait: "If ever there should be a monastery without an awkward and ill-tempered member, it would be necessary to go and find one and pay him his weight in gold—so great is the profit that results from this trial, when it is used properly." In other words, we should never underestimate the potential benefit of engaging successfully with a colleague with whom we find it difficult to work.

919   **Mutual respect** "But we appeal to you, brothers and sisters, to respect those who labor among you." Paul the apostle extended this teaching to every level of work, including those who "have charge of you ... and admonish you." They have their task to fulfill for the common good, so "esteem them very highly in love because of their work" (1 Thessalonians 5:12–13).

---

920 ONE BODY, MANY MEMBERS

In his letter to the Corinthians, Paul the apostle taught the importance of recognizing the value of every member of the community (1 Corinthians 12:12–26). He likened the community to the human body, which "does not consist of one member but of many." Within the body, each individual part performs a crucial function and is as important as all the other parts: "The eye cannot say to the hand, 'I have no need of you,' nor the head to the feet, 'I have no need of you.'" However weak some members of a community seem to be, they should nevertheless be regarded as "indispensable." And to ensure that everyone "may have the same care for one another," God has "arranged" the community in such a way that in "giving the greater honor to the inferior member ... there may be no dissension within the body, but the members may have the same care for one another. If one member suffers, all suffer together with it; if one member is honored, all rejoice together with it" (24–26).

---

921   Working principle "In everything do to others as you would have them do to you; for this is the law and the prophets."
MATTHEW 7:12

922   Breakdown in communication The famous saying "the left hand does not know what the right hand is doing" is derived from the Sermon on the Mount (Matthew 6:3). Although on that occasion Jesus was referring to giving alms in secret, the expression has become an idiom in the modern world for lack of communication, especially in large organizations.

923 **The tax collector** One of Jesus' disciples was Matthew, a
tax collector. Men of his profession were paid by the Romans
and were known for lining their pockets through bribery and
extortion. Tax collectors were despised by the Jews who looked
upon them as no better than sinners. There was no pride to be
felt in their work, and it is unlikely that Matthew was happy in
his job. So when Jesus said to him, "Follow me" (Matthew 9:9),
he jumped at the opportunity to be a disciple of Christ and join
his community, and immediately abandoned his dishonest trade.
Integrity and honest dealing are pre-requisites of following Christ.

---

924 **SHINE YOUR LIGHT**
When we have done something good and
worthwhile, Christ taught we should not be
modest and conceal it since everyone stands to
benefit from what we have produced: "Let your
light shine before others, so that they may see
your good works" (Matthew 5:16).

925 **Union of minds** "Every citizen should have a voice in the conduct of the business or industry which is carried on by means of his labour, and the satisfaction of knowing that his labour is directed to the well-being of the community."
WILLIAM TEMPLE (1881–1944), ENGLAND

926 **Young and old** The Scottish writer and Christian minister George MacDonald (1824–1905) was of the belief that "When we are out of sympathy with the young, then ... our work in this world is over."

927 **Self-control** Working in a team can try the patience at times, but the wise person will avoid losing their temper to prevent unpleasant ramifications: "Like a city breached, without walls, is one who lacks self-control."
PROVERBS 25:28

928 **Work hard for all** "Make all you can, save all you can, give all you can."
JOHN WESLEY (1703–1791), ENGLAND

929 **Together before God** "We do not live to ourselves, and we do not die to ourselves. If we live, we live to the Lord, and if we die, we die to the Lord"
ROMANS 14:7–8

---

930 **HUMAN AUTHORITY**
The relationship between Christians and earthly authority has been the subject of considerable debate over the years. Although the Bible does not stipulate any particular form of government, it does demand that whatever form it takes, it should be just. As the apostle Paul says in his letter to the Roman Christians, "Let every person be subject to the governing authorities; for there is no authority except from God, and those authorities that exist have been instituted by God" (Romans 13:1). The ultimate source of all authority is God, so if we believe the human authorities conflict with the word of God, then we

[345]

are within our rights to protest, as did the apostles Peter and John during the council in Jerusalem: "For we cannot keep from speaking about what we have seen and heard" (Acts 4:20).

---

931 **Doing good deeds** "Good works [deeds] are the most perfect when they are wrought in the most pure and sincere love of God, and with the least regard to our own present and future interests, or to joy and sweetness, consolation or praise."
ST. JOHN OF THE CROSS (1542–1591), SPAIN

932 **Ordained way of life** The author of Psalms considered work to be a part of God's order in creation: "People go out to their work and to their labor until the evening."
PSALM 104:23

933 **Wholehearted application** "Whatever your task, put yourselves into it, as done for the Lord and not for your masters."
COLOSSIANS 3:23

934   **Virtue in work** "Thank God—every morning when you get up—that you have something to do which must be done, whether you like it or not. Being forced to work, and forced to do your best, will breed in you a hundred virtues which the idle never know."
CHARLES KINGSLEY (1819 1875), ENGLAND

935   **Brace up and knuckle down** "Arouse yourself, gird your loins, put aside idleness, grasp the nettle and do some hard work."
ST. BERNARD OF CLAIRVAUX (1090–1153), FRANCE

936   **Living in harmony** The apostle Paul taught in his epistle to the Romans that we were created to live in harmony with each other, each complementing the other's activity: "For as in one body we have many members, and not all the members have the same function, so we, who are many, are one body in Christ, and individually we are members one of another. We have gifts that differ according to the grace given to us" (Romans 12:4–6).

937   **Bear one another's burdens** "It is the part of a Christian to take care of his own body for the very purpose that, by its

soundness and wellbeing, he may be enabled to labor, and to acquire and preserve property, for the aid of those who are in want; that thus the stronger member may serve the weaker member, and we may be children of God, thoughtful and busy one for another, bearing one another's burdens, and so fulfilling the law of Christ."
MARTIN LUTHER (1483–1546), GERMANY

938   **Sustained effort** "O Lord God, when Thou givest to Thy servants to endeavour any great matter, grant us to know that it is not the beginning but the continuing of the same until it be thoroughly finished, which yieldeth the true glory."
SIR FRANCIS DRAKE (c. 1540–c. 1596), ENGLAND

939   **In the workplace** The apostle Paul taught that whatever misfortunes we suffer, we must keep from falling out with each other: "Be at peace among yourselves" (1 Thessalonians 5:13).

940   **Building together** In the Old Testament, the Israelite leader Nehemiah tells how his people were frequently attacked while building the new walls of Jerusalem. But he organized them so efficiently that they were able to work together productively while at the same time protecting each other. (Nehemiah 4:16–21.)

941 **Teamwork** "The great cannot exist without the less, nor the less without the great."
ST. CLEMENT OF ROME (DIED c. 99), ITALY

942 **Support the less able** "Let the weaker be helped so that they may not do their work in sadness."
ST. BENEDICT OF NURSIA (c. 480–c. 543), ITALY

TRAVEL

943   Patron of travelers The legend of St. Christopher, patron of travelers, tells of a man who puts his strength to good use by helping travelers cross a river. On one occasion, he assists a child through the water, but he proves so heavy that Christopher cries out that he feels as though he is carrying the whole world on his shoulders. "You are," answered the boy, "And him who made it." Christopher (meaning "Christ bearer") then realized he was carrying Christ on his shoulders—and the burden lifted immediately. The story of this saint is often remembered by those who feel their burdens in life are too great—in Christ they become easier to bear.

944   Keep faith
"My path is lost; my wandring [sic] steps do stray;
I cannot safely go, nor safely stay;
Whom should I see but Thee,
My Path, my Way?"
FRANCIS QUARLES (1592–1644), ENGLAND

945   Into the unknown Sometimes, without necessarily knowing why, we feel the need to turn away from our familiar environment and move on. As in the story of Abraham in Genesis, the matter becomes one of faith: "Now the Lord said to Abraham, 'Go from your country and your kindred and your father's house to the land that I will show you'" (Genesis 12:1). Abraham did not know where God was leading him, but he knew he must obey the divine command. As the author of Hebrews reminds us: "By faith, Abraham obeyed when he was called to set out ... not knowing where he was going" (Hebrews 11:18).

946   **Slowly but surely** "It is the same with people who travel: if they tire themselves out on the very first day by rushing along, they will end up wasting many days as a result of sickness. But if they start out walking at a gentle pace until they have got accustomed to walking, in the end they will not get tired, even though they walk great distances."
EVAGRIUS OF PONTUS (c. 346–399), ASIA MINOR (TURKEY)

947   **The Pilgrim Fathers** In 1620 a band of 102 Christians who wished to settle in a new land where they could practice their

faith without hindrance set sail on an English ship, the *Mayflower*, bound for America. After a journey lasting ten weeks, the pilgrims still had "all things to doe, as in the beginning of the world." Despite the harsh winter and food shortages, there were enough survivors to found a colony, which was named after the port from which they set sail—Plymouth. Their firm conviction in God's protection was strong enough to see them through the difficult times. As with any venture into the unknown, faith and determination will put you on the right track.

948 PILGRIMAGE

A pilgrimage is a journey to a sacred site to acquire knowledge, to be spiritually or physically cleansed, or to express religious devotion. For many, it is a metaphor for life— the journey we set out on from the day we are born on the road to the Otherworld. The earliest Christians ventured to the Holy Land to visit the places of Christ's life and Passion, and in the Middle Ages, pilgrims were able to travel throughout Europe to see the tombs of saints and their relics. The modern pilgrim leaves behind normal life to travel to a specific site, often in search of spiritual replenishment. In 1992, Archbishop George Carey (1991–2002), for example, led a thousand Anglicans to the ecumenical monastic community at Taizé, France, because of its significance as "a place of generosity and reconciliation."

---

949 **Spiritual trading** "Impart as much as you can of your spiritual being to those who are on the road with you, and accept as something precious what comes back to you from them."
ALBERT SCHWEITZER (1875–1965), GERMANY

950 **Source of wisdom** St. Augustine of Hippo (354–430) traveled around the Mediterranean region extensively, and did much of his thinking and writing during that time. Interacting with different people and cultures broadened his mind: "The World is a book," he said, "and those who do not travel read only a page."

951   Essentials for a pilgrimage

"Give me my Scallop shell of quiet,

My staffe of Faith to walke upon,

My Scrip [scripture] of Joy, Immortall diet,

My bottle of salvation:

My Gowne of Glory, hope's true gage,

And thus Ile take my pilgrimage."

SIR WALTER RALEIGH (c. 1554–1618), ENGLAND

952   Travel is a teacher

"An inexperienced person knows
    few things,

and one with much experience
    knows what he is talking
    about.

I have seen many things in my
    travels,

and I understand more than I
    can express."

ECCLESIASTICUS 34:10–12

953 To be a pilgrim

"There's no discouragement
Shall make him once relent
His first avow'd intent
To be a pilgrim."
JOHN BUNYAN (1628–1688), ENGLAND

954 A symbol of life "We see in these swift and skillful travelers [pilgrims] a symbol of our life, which seeks to be a pilgrimage and a passage on this earth for the way of heaven."
POPE PAUL VI (1963–1978), ITALY

955 No entry

"Do not enter the path of the wicked,
and do not walk in the way of
    evildoers.
Avoid it; do not go on it;
    turn away from it and pass on."
PROVERBS 4:14–17

956 PAUL'S MISSIONARY JOURNEYS
The journeys of the apostle Paul throughout the Roman empire took him into contact with people of many different cultures and faiths in what was largely a pagan world. He faced many perils on his wanderings: "Three times I was shipwrecked; for a night and a day I was

adrift at sea; on frequent journeys, in danger from rivers, danger from bandits, danger from my own people, danger from Gentiles, danger in the city, danger in the wilderness, danger at sea, danger from false brothers and sisters; in toil and hardship, through many a sleepless night, hungry and thirsty, often without food, cold and naked" (2 Corinthians 11:25–27). But Paul bore his trials with equanimity, spurred on by his resolve to lay the foundations of the church in Europe.

---

957   **Thrill of going**

"Exultation is the going
Of an inland soul to sea—
Past the houses, past the headlands,
Into deep Eternity!

Bred as we, among the mountains,
Can the sailor understand

The divine intoxication
Of the first league out from land?"
EMILY DICKINSON (1830–1886), USA

958   **No hope?** The account in the Book of Exodus of the Israelites
wandering in the wilderness, not knowing where their next meal
would come from or how long their journey might take, teaches
that God will provide for us, however desperate the situation:
"Morning by morning they gathered it [bread], as much as each
needed; but when the sun grew hot it melted" (Exodus 16:21).
When they were hungry, God showered them with manna from
heaven; when thirsty, they came upon a hidden aquifer. Often,
as in the biblical example, after a journey has begun and
problems arise, help seems to come completely unexpectedly,
as if from nowhere.

959   **Crown of thorns** "... I rose early, before sunrise ... and rambled
off to the holy places on Mount Sion ... and on the Mount
of Olives.... I gathered some of the thorns which grow in the
hedges on the side of the Mount of Olives, and of the Mount

Sion, and I bound twigs of them together, and wove them into a crown of thorns in the way, and of the thorns wherewith I believe that the Lord Jesus was crowned."

BROTHER FELIX FABRI (c. 1441–1502), SWITZERLAND

960 **To the ends of the earth** The Scottish missionary explorer Dr. Livingstone (1813–1873) felt compelled to follow Jesus' directive to "make disciples of all nations" (Matthew 28:19) by taking the gospel deep into Africa. Conducting several explorations, on foot, he crossed the entire continent over a period of 30 years. But he made light of the effort: "The effect of travel on a man whose heart is in the right place is that the mind is made more self-reliant: it becomes more confident of its own resources…. The sweat of one's brow is no longer a curse when one works for God: it proves a tonic to the system, and actually a blessing."

PEACE

961   **Christ's example** A recurrent theme of Christ's ministry on
Earth was the call for his followers not only to seek inner, spiritual
peace but to become peacemakers. His famous words, "Blessed
are the peacemakers, for they will be called children of God"
(Matthew 5:9), is one of many biblical passages urging believers
to follow the path of peace rather than that of violence or
confrontation. Even at times of extreme tension, Christ's message
is clear: in the full knowledge that he is soon to be put to death,
he comforts his disciples, **"Peace I leave with you; my peace
I give to you" (962)** (John 14:27); again, during his arrest and
prior to his Crucifixion, his last instruction to the apostle Peter is
"Put your sword back in its place; for **all who take the sword
will perish by the sword" (963)** (Matthew 26:52).

964   **Piety and peace** "We must divide all the children of Adam into
two classes: the first belong to the kingdom of God, the second to
the kingdom of the world ... The one to produce piety, the other
to bring about external peace and prevent evil deeds; neither is
sufficient in the world without the other."
MARTIN LUTHER (1483–1546), GERMANY

965 **Nuclear giants, ethical infants** "We have grasped the mystery of the atom and rejected the Sermon on the Mount. Ours is a world of nuclear giants and ethical infants. We know more about war than we know about peace, more about killing than we know about living."

GENERAL OMAR BRADLEY (1893–1981), USA

966 **Laying down arms**

"They shall beat their swords into
    plowshares,
and their spears into pruning
    hooks;
nation shall not lift up sword
    against nation
neither shall they learn war
    any more."

ISAIAH 2:4

967 **Invite peace** "Make peace with yourself and heaven and earth will make peace with you. Endeavor to enter your own inner cell,

and you will see the heavens, because the one and the other are
one and the same, and when you enter one you see the two."
ISAAC OF NINEVEH (7th CENTURY), SYRIA

968   Peace within "Honor peace more than anything else. But strive
first of all to be at peace in yourself."
JOHN OF APAMEA (6th CENTURY), SYRIA

969   Consideration for others In his letter to the Romans,
Paul talked about the eating habits within a mixed ethnic
group. Some were offended at the sight of meat that had
been used for sacrificial purposes. He enjoined his church
to be considerate toward the feelings of others and to
"pursue what makes for peace and for mutual upbuilding"
(Romans 14:19).

970   The peace of God "And the peace of God, which surpasses
all understanding, shall guard your hearts and your minds in
Christ Jesus."
PHILIPPIANS 4:7 [KJV]

971   Four Quartets

"I said to my soul, be still and wait without hope
For hope would be hope for the wrong thing; wait without love
For love would be love of the wrong thing; there is yet faith
But the faith and the love and the hope are all in the waiting.
Wait without thought, for you are not ready for the thought:
So the darkness shall be the light, and the stillness the dancing.
T.S. ELIOT (1888–1965), USA/ENGLAND

972   **Inner peace** "Thou madest us for Thyself, and our heart is restless until it repose in Thee."
ST. AUGUSTINE OF HIPPO (354–430), NORTH AFRICA

973   **Yourself first** "Keep thyself first in peace, and then shalt thou be able to pacify others. A peaceable man doth more good than he that is well."
THOMAS À KEMPIS (c.1380–1471), GERMANY

974   **At work in us** "Peace and love are always at work in us, but we are not always in peace and love."
MOTHER JULIAN OF NORWICH (1342–c. 1416), ENGLAND

975   **Nobel Peace Prize** The Swedish scientist Alfred Nobel (1833–1896) invented dynamite but was also, perhaps surprisingly, a man of peace. To encourage this attitude, in 1895 he gifted The Nobel Peace Prize, to be awarded each year to those who further the cause of world peace. In 1964 it was presented to pastor **Martin Luther King, Jr. (976)** (1929–1968), leader of the Southern Christian Leadership Conference, in acknowledgment of his tremendous contribution as a campaigner for civil rights. And In 1979, **Mother Teresa of Calcutta (977)** (1910–1997) received the Nobel prize for her example of love for society's outcasts. In her acceptance speech she said, "I am grateful to receive [the Nobel] in the name of the hungry, the naked, the homeless, of the crippled, of the blind, of the lepers, of all those people who feel unwanted, unloved, uncared-for throughout society, people that have become a burden to the society and are shunned by everyone.... Every act of love is a work of peace, no matter how small."

978   **Channel of thy peace** "Lord, make me a channel of thy peace —that where there is hatred, I may bring love—that where there is wrong, I may bring the spirit of forgiveness—that where there is discord, I may bring harmony—that where there is error, I may bring truth—that where there is doubt, I may bring faith—that where there is despair, I may bring hope—that where there are shadows, I may bring light—that where there is sadness, I may bring joy."
ST. FRANCIS OF ASSISI (c. 1182–1226), ITALY

979   **Never through violence** "Peace cannot be achieved through violence, it can only be attained through understanding."
RALPH WALDO EMERSON (1803–1882), USA

980   **True blessedness** "What is more suitable and appropriate to true blessedness than an eternity of peace and joy?"
ST. JOHN CASSIAN (360–435), SCYTHIA

981   **Follow God's will** "In his will is our peace."
DANTE (1265–1321), ITALY

982   **In your heart** "Keep your heart in peace; let nothing in this world disturb it: everything has an end."
ST. JOHN OF THE CROSS (1542–1591), SPAIN

983   **Of the holy angels and saints** "The perfect peace of the holy angels lies in their love for God and their love for one another. This is also the case with all the saints from the beginning of time."
MAXIMUS THE CONFESSOR (c. 580–662), GREECE

984 Quiet in our souls

"Drop thy still dews of quietness,
Till all our strivings cease;
Take from our souls the strain and stress,
And let our ordered lives confess
The beauty of thy peace."
JOHN WHITTIER (1807–1892), USA

985 Reconciliation "For he [Christ] is our peace; in his flesh he has made both groups into one and has broken down the dividing wall, that is, the hostility between us" (Ephesians 2:14). When two clans or groups are opposed to each other, as were the Jews and Gentiles in New Testament times, it is the loving spirit of Christ that can settle their differences, and "... create in himself one new humanity in place of the two, thus making peace, and ... [reconciling] both groups to God in one body through the cross, thus putting to death that hostility...." (Ephesians 2:15–16).

986 Fruit of the Spirit "[T]he fruit of the Spirit is love, joy, peace...."
GALATIANS 5:22

987   **The wicked** "'There is no peace,' says the Lord, 'for the wicked.'"
ISAIAH 48:22

988   **Prayer for peace** "O God, from whom all holy desires, all good counsels, and all just works do proceed; Give unto thy servants that peace which the world cannot give."
BOOK OF COMMON PRAYER (1662), ENGLAND

989   **If only...** Although the medieval mystic St. Bridget of Sweden (1303–1373) was intent on leading a quiet monastic life, she nevertheless had a considerable talent for diplomacy and helped in the delicate negotiations to bring Pope Blessed Urban V (1362–1370) back to Rome from exile in Avignon, France. The difficulties she faced made her once declare: "The world would have peace if the men of politics would only follow the gospel."

990   **Amid the urban squeeze**
"Calm soul of all things, make it mine
To feel amid the city's jar

That there exists a peace of thine
Man did not make and cannot mar."
MATTHEW ARNOLD (1822–1888), ENGLAND

991   Despite ourselves "To thee, O God, we turn for peace … but grant us too the blessed assurance that nothing shall deprive us of that peace, neither ourselves, nor our foolish earthly desires, nor my wild longings, nor the anxious cravings of my heart."
SØREN KIERKEGAARD (1813–1855), DENMARK

992   Do the will of others "My son, now will I teach thee the way of peace and inward liberty. Be desirous to do the will of another rather than thine own. Choose always to have less rather than more.... Wish always, and pray, that the will of God may be wholly fulfilled in thee."
THOMAS À KEMPIS (c. 1380–1471), GERMANY

993   Shadow of sin The English novelist George Eliot (1819–1880), famous for *Middlemarch* and *Silas Marner*, was interested in the complex religious and moral attitudes of her time, which caused

998 **Turning a blind eye** "Who ever winks the eye causes trouble, but the one who rebukes boldly makes peace."
PROVERBS 10:10

999 **Sincerity** "While you are proclaiming peace with your lips, be careful to have it even more fully in your heart."
ST. FRANCIS OF ASSISI (c. 1182–1226), ITALY

1000 **The faithful** "The most faithful disciples of Christ have been builders of peace, to the point of forgiving their enemies, sometimes even to the point of giving their lives for them."
POPE JOHN PAUL II (1978–2005)

1001 **A simple smile** "Peace begins with a smile—smile a hundred times a day at someone you don't really feel like smiling at—do it for peace. In this way we will spread the peace of God, and in this way we will shine with His light, and in the world and in the hearts of men we will snuff out all hatred and all love of power."
MOTHER TERESA (1910–1997), INDIA

FURTHER READING

(Anonymous.) *The Cloud of Unknowing.* (1370.) London: John M. Watkins, 1922.

Adels, Jill. *The Wisdom of the Saints.* Oxford: Oxford University Press (OUP), 1987.

Aquinas, Thomas. *Summa Theologiae.* (60 vols, Latin text and English translations.) London: Black Friers, in conjunction with Eyre & Spottiswoode, no date.

Augustine, Bishop of Hippo. *Confessions.* Trans. by E.B. Pusey. Oxford: J.H. Parker, 1840.

Augustine, Bishop of Hippo. *Enchiridion.* Trans. by J.F. Shaws. London: Religious Tract Society, 1887.

Augustine, Bishop of Hippo. *The City of God.* Trans. by Rev. Marcus Dods. Edinburgh: Clark, 1878.

Barclay, William. *The Daily Study Bible.* (17 vols.) London: Westminster John Knox Press, 1979.

Barton, J, and Muddiman, J. (eds.) *The Oxford Bible Commentary.* Oxford: OUP, 2001.

Benedict, St. *The Holy Rule of St. Benedict.* Trans. by a Priest of Mount Mellaray. London: T. Richardson & Son, 1865.

Bernard of Clairvaux. *The Twelve Degrees of Humility and Pride.* Trans. by Barton R.V. Mills. London: SPCK, 1929.

Bettenson, Henry. (ed. and trans.) *The Early Christian Fathers.* Oxford: OUP, 1956.

Bettenson, Henry. (ed. and trans.) *The Later Christian Fathers.* Oxford: OUP, 1956.

Bonhoeffer, Dietrich. *The Cost of Discipleship.* London: SCM Press, 1948.

Bonhoeffer, Dietrich. *Letters & Papers from Prison.* Trans. by Reginald H.Fuller. London: SCM Press, 1953.

Catherine of Siena. *The Dialogue.* Trans. by Algar Thorold. London: Burns, Oates & Washbourne, 1925.

Church of England, *The Book of Common Prayer from the Original Manuscript Attached to the Act of Uniformity of 1662, and now preserved in the House of Lords.* London: Eyre & Spottiswoode, 1892.

Cox, Michael. *A Handbook of Christian Mysticism.* London: Aquarian Press, 1986.

Day, Malcolm. *A Treasury of Saints.* New York: Barron's, 2002.

Eckhart, Meister. *Sermons.* Trans. by Claud Field. London: Heart & Life Booklets, 1903.

Emerson, Ralph Waldo. *The Conduct of Life.* London: G. Bell & Sons, 1883.

Erasmus, Desiderius. *In Praise of Folly.* London: Allen & Unwin, 1915.

Francis of Assisi. *His life and writings as recorded by his contemporaries.* Trans. by Leo Sherley-Price. London: A.R. Mowbray, 1959.

Gibran, Kahlil. *Kahlil Gibran's The Prophet and The Art of Peace.* London: Duncan Baird Publishers, 2008.

Griffin, Emilie. (ed.) *Francis and Clare of Assisi: Selected Writings.* Translated by Armstrong and Brady. London: HarperCollins, 2006.

Harris, Paul. (ed.) *The Fire of Silence and Stillness.* London: Darton, Longman and Todd, 1995.

Harpur, James. *Love Burning in the Soul.* Boston: Shambhala Publications, 2005.

Harvey, A.E. *A Companion to the New Testament.* Cambridge: Cambridge University Press (CUP), 1970.

Ignatius of Loyola. *The Spiritual Exercises.* London: Burns, Oates & Washbourne, 1881.

John of the Cross. *The Collected Works.* (1577–1585.) Trans. by Kieran Kavanaugh and Otilio Rodriguez. London: Nelson,1966.

Julian of Norwich. *Sixteen Revelations of Divine Love.* London: H.R. Allenson, 1911.

à Kempis, Thomas. *The Imitation of Christ.* London: Elliott Stock, 1893.

Lane, Tony. *A Concise History of Christian Thought.* London: Continuum, 2006.

Lewis, C.S. *Miracles.* London: Fontana, 1947 (1960, revised).

Lewis, C.S. *Mere Christianity.* London: Fontana, 1955.

Lewis, C.S. *Christian Reflections.* London: Geoffrey Bles, 1967.

Lightfoot, R.H. *St John's Gospel: A Commentary.* Oxford: Clarendon Press, 1956.

Luther, Martin. *First Principles of the Reformation: The ninety-five theses and the three primary works of Martin Luther.* By R.S. Grignon. Theological introductions by H. Wace. London: John Murray, 1883.

Merton, Thomas. *The Seven Storey Mountain.* New York: Harcourt, Brace & Co, 1948.

More, Thomas. *Utopia.* Trans. by Ralphe Robynson. London: Ashendene Press, Chelsea, 1906.

Niebuhr, Reihold. *Leaves from the Notebook of a Tamed Cynic.* Chicago: Willett, Clark & Colby, 1929.

Niebuhr, Reihold. *Nature and Destiny of Man.* Nisbet, 1943.

Rowley, H.H. *Dictionary of Bible Themes.* London: Thomas Nelson, 1968.

Scrivener, Frederick Henry Ambrose.*The Authorized Edition of the English Bible, 1611, its subsequent reprints and modern representatives.* Cambridge: Cambridge University Press, 1884.

Smith, Robert. *A Quaker Book of Wisdom.* London: Victor Gollancz, 1998.

Temple, William. *Christianity and the Social Order.* London: Penguin, 1942.

Teresa of Avila. *The Complete Works.* (3 Vols.) Trans. and edited by E. Allison Peers. London: Sheed & Ward, 1944–1946.

Tertullian. *The Writings of Tertullian.* Trans. by S. Thelwall, P. Holmes and others in vols 3 & 4 of *Ante-Nicene Fathers.* University of Edinburgh: Edinburgh 1869

Underhill, Evelyn. *Mysticism.* London: Methuen & Co, 1911.

Ward, Benedicta. (ed. and trans.) *Sayings of the Desert Fathers.* London: Macmillan, 1980.

Wesley, John. *Journal.* London: Isaac Pitman and Sons, 1905.

Wiles, Maurice. *The Christian Fathers.* London: Hodder and Stoughton, 1966.

INDEX

Note: References in the index are page numbers.

Abelard, Peter 131
Abraham 70, 351
Adam 23, 24, 27–28, 265
Addison, Joseph 59, 117, 222
Aelred of Rievaulx, St. 249, 324
Alphonsus Liguori, St. 238
Ambrose, St. 33, 156, 265
Amos 205–207
Angela Merici, St. 189
Angela of Foligno 120, 161, 165
angels 68–84, 254
    angel of the Lord 74, 82
    guardian angels 74–75, 76
    hierarchy 71
    rebel angels 78
Annunciation 80
Anselm, St. 156, 238
Anthony of Egypt, St. 11, 127, 234
Aquinas, St. Thomas 20, 34–35, 77, 94, 117, 137, 175, 191, 196, 371
archangels 73
Arnold, Johann Christoph 310
Arnold, Matthew 370
Ascension of Christ 61
Athanasius, St. 90
Augustine of Hippo, St. 7, 27, 45–46, 63, 91, 94, 96, 103, 108, 122, 128, 140, 147, 154, 155, 157, 170, 171, 182, 190, 217, 220, 244, 258, 263, 265, 268, 315, 326, 354, 365

Bacon, Francis 79–80, 129
baptism 31–32, 167, 290
Barclay, William 41
Barth, Karl 223
Basil of Caesarea, St. 320, 329
Basil the Great, St. 197
Baxter, Richard 301, 302
Beatitudes, the 210–212
Bede the Venerable, St. 326
Beecher, Henry Ward 144
Bellarmine, Robert 62
Benedict of Nursia, St. 229, 280, 349
Benson, Robert 182
Berdyaev, Nikolai 188
Bernard of Clairvaux, St. 91–92, 113, 117, 168, 169, 228, 233, 339, 347
Blake, William 48, 50, 145, 263
Blount, Sir Thomas Pope 20
Boehme, Jakob 48, 65
Bonaventure 86, 134, 230

Bonhoeffer, Dietrich 93, 152, 175, 183, 224
Boulard, Henri 154
Bowles, William Lisle 271
Bradley, Omar (Gen.) 11, 362
Bridget of Sweden, St. 369
Bronte, Emily 66
Browning, Elizabeth Barrett 233
Brueggemann, Walter 276
Bunyan, John 94–95, 237, 356
Burke, Edmund 171

Cabasilas, Nicolas 32
Cain and Abel 304–305
Calvin, John 10, 25, 93, 104, 135, 203
Camus, Jean Pierre 137, 263
Cardenal, Ernesto 17
Carey, George (Archbishop) 354
Carlyle, Thomas 154, 219
Catherine of Genoa, St. 62
Catherine of Siena, St. 36, 43–44, 228, 332–333
Caussade, Jean-Pierre de 15
Celestial Hierarchy 71
Chambers, Oswald 28, 186, 235

Chantal, Jeanne Françoise
de 250
Chapman, Robert Cleaver
234
Chardin, Pierre Teilhard de
48, 315
childbirth 282–287
children 302–310
Choan-Seng Song 282
Christopher, St. 350
Chromatius of Aquileia, St.
136
Clare of Assisi, St. 11, 193,
197, 257, 286
Claver, Peter 159
Clement of Alexandria, St.
89, 126
Clement of Rome, St. 349
Cloud of Unknowing, The
46, 59
Coleridge, Samuel Taylor
235, 271
confession 146–157
Cornelius the centurion 218
courage 172–182
Covenant, The 138, 313–314
Cowper, William 130, 322
Creation 14–22
Crescenzo, Luciano de 372
Cross, The 119
crusaders 175–176
Cuyler, Theodore Ledyard 310
Cyprian, St. 104–105
Cyril of Jerusalem, St. 101

Dali, Salvador 20
Daniel 240–241
Dante 367
David and Goliath 174
Day of Judgement 64
Denck, Hans 266–267
Dickens, Charles 276
Dickinson, Emily 358–359
Donne, John 66–67, 153,
240, 291, 319
Doolittle, Antoinette 204
Dorotheus of Gaza, St. 326
Dostoyevsky, Fyodor 33, 124
doubt 255–262
Drake, Sir Francis 348
Dryden, John 191
duty 183–189

Eckhart, Meister 74, 129,
237, 283
Eden, Garden of 26
Edmund the Martyr, St.
233–234
Eggleston, Edward 310
Einstein, Albert 33
Elijah 244
Eliot, George 370–371
Eliot, T.S. 280, 364
Ellis, Henry Havelock 34
Emerson, Ralph Waldo 14,
79, 158, 209, 367
endurance 157–162
Ephraem the Syrian, St. 137,
232, 249

Epiphany 36–37
Erskine, Ralph 255
Eucharist 104
Eusebius of Caesarea 92
Evagrius of Pontus 351
Eve 24, 28, 265, 286
Exodus 266
Ezekiel 117, 202

Faber, Frederick William 45,
158, 188
Fabri, Brother Felix 359–360
faith 112, 119, 126, 172,
179, 209, 217–226,
255–262
Fall of Man 27–28
feeding the 5,000 239–240
Fénelon, François 163, 188
Flavel, John 226, 297–298
Flood 29–32, 138
forgiveness 138–145
fortitude 172–182
Fox, George 48–50, 371–372
Fox, Matthew 172–173
Francis of Assisi, St. 8, 11, 21,
46–48, 71, 112, 114,
128, 162, 209, 252,
320, 366, 373
Francis of Sales, St. 47, 68,
74, 162, 225, 250, 254
Francis Xavier, St. 309, 325
free will 263–265
freedom 263–271
friendship 318–325

377

Fromm, Erich 127
Frost, Robert 143, 277
Fulgentius of Ruspe, St. 125
Fuller, Thomas 322
Furlong, Monica 111

Gabriel 73, 80, 82
Gandhi, Mahatma 42
Gethsemane 185, 235–237
Gibran, Kahlil 303, 319
Giles of Assisi, St. 335
Giocondo, Fra Giovanni 225
Gladstone, William 280
Goblin Market 323
Goliath 174
Gonzaga, Aloysius 63
Good Samaritan 330
Grace 94–105
Gregory I, Pope 83, 91,
    161–162, 257
Gregory of Nazianzus, St. 127
guardian angels 74–75, 76
guilt 146
Gurney, Dorothy Frances
    281, 298

Habakkuk 257–258
"Hail Mary" prayer 238
Hamilton, James 274
Heaven 52–67
Henry, Matthew 24, 54, 103,
    183, 233, 237
Herbert, George 157,
    253–254

Hildegard of Bingen, St.
    44
Hodge, Charles 261
Holland, Josiah Gilbert 282
Holy Spirit 92, 98–99, 101,
    251–252
home life 274–281
Hopkins, Gerard Manley 39
Hopkins, John Henry 162
Horozco, Juan de 156
Hosea 119
Hugo, Victor 182
humankind 23
humility 163–171

Incarnation 89, 287
Ignatius of Loyola, St. 103,
    183, 225, 254
Immaculate Conception 285
inspiration 249–254
Interior Castle, The 38
Introduction to the Devout
    Life 47
Irenaeus, St. 23, 249
Isaac of Nineveh 232–233,
    362–363
Isaiah 122–123, 203
Isidore of Seville, St. 105,
    322–323

Jacob 73, 293, 306, 311
Jairus's daughter 308
Jeremiah 201, 203
Jericho 241–243

Jesus
    as prophet 208
    Ascension 61
    conception and birth
        80–83, 282–287
    Crucifixion 119
    denied by Peter 150
    entry into Jerusalem 164–165
    Gethsemane, Garden of
        185, 236–237
    grace in childhood 98
    Last Supper 104, 167, 176
    Mary and Martha 187–188
    ministry 209–216
    miracles 239–240, 243–
        244, 245, 247–248, 299,
        308
    parables 56–58, 191–193,
        213, 231, 276–277, 330
    Passion 176
    return 218–219
    Sermon on the Mount
        210–212, 341
    stigmata 46
    Temptations in the desert
        258–260
    Transfiguration 40–41
Jesus Prayer 51
Job 7, 161
John XXIII, Pope 111
John Cassian, St. 367
John Chrysostom, St. 101,
    153, 162, 163, 251,
    265, 274

378

John of Alvernia 116
John of Apamea 363
John of Bosco, St. 74
John of Damascus, St. 19, 84
John of the Cross, St. 43, 128,
    261–262, 346, 367
John Paul II, Pope 181, 373
John the Baptist 82, 147
Johnson, Paul 287
Jonah 207
Jophiel 73
Joseph 305–306
Joshua 175
Julian of Norwich 22, 118,
    222, 231, 365
Jung, Carl 245
Justin Martyr, St. 90, 181

Kagawa, Toyohiko 244
Kant, Immanuel 56, 185 186
Keble, John 250
Kelly, Thomas 88
Kempe, Margery 234
Kempis, Thomas à 58, 95,
    124, 170, 196, 248,
    260, 270, 329, 335,
    365, 370
Kierkegaard, Søren 11, 88,
    111, 132 134, 145,
    238, 370
kindness 127
King, Martin Luther 365–366
Kingsley, Charles 189, 266,
    304, 347

Kung, Hans 65

Lactantius, Lucius 204
Last Judgment 64
Last Supper 104, 167, 176
Law, William 112, 232
Lawrence, Brother (Nicolas
    Herman) 48
Lazarus 214, 243–244
Leviathan 20
Lewis, C.S. 17, 62, 64, 156,
    171, 186, 260, 336–337
light 18–19, 20
Lightfoot, Dr. John 15
Lightfoot, R.H. 18
Lincoln, Abraham 186
Linné, Carl von 25
Livingstone, Dr. 360
Locke, John 33
Longfellow, Henry Wadsworth
    67, 75
Lord's Prayer 227
Lot 69
love 33, 65, 115, 116,
    118–128
Lucifer 78–79
Luther, Martin 10, 14, 17,
    29, 84, 126, 223–224,
    225, 258, 267, 298,
    330–332, 335, 337–338,
    347–348, 361

MacDonald, George 337, 344
Magi 36–37, 130, 290

Magna Carta 269
Main, John 37
marriage 292–301
martyrs 180–181
Mary and Martha 187–188
Mary of Egypt, St. 88–89
materialism 213, 214–215
Matthew, St. 342
Maurice, F.D. 227
Maximus the Confessor, St.
    91, 367
McDowell, Josh 302
McKenzie, J.L. 205
Melville, Herman 261
Merton, Thomas 34, 187,
    255, 269, 318
Messiah 203, 313–314
Michael 73
Milton, John 20, 68, 80, 269
miracles 239–248, 299, 308
Mirror of Simple Souls 42–43
Moore, Thomas 67
More, Thomas 181
Moses 75, 109, 112, 118,
    175, 212, 247, 313
mysticism 34, 36, 38–51, 74,
    204–205
    mystic wedding 43–44

Nature 15, 17, 20, 21, 25,
    158
    mysticism 47–51
Nehemiah 348–349
neighborliness 326–338

379

Newbigin, Lesslie 257
Newman, John Henry 189, 219, 226, 261
Newton, John 99–100
Nicaean Creed 229
Nicholas of Flüe, St. 94
Niebuhr, Reinhold 182
Niebuhr, Ursula 154
Niemoller, Martin 149
Nightingale, Florence 8, 39–40, 173
Noah 29, 31, 96, 138, 311
Nobel, Alfred 365
Nouwen, Henri 277–278
numinousness 42

obedience 117
On Religion 34
O'Neill, Eugene 100
Origen of Alexandria 271
Otto, Rudolf 41–42
Oxyrhynchus Sayings of Jesus 61

Pachomius 324
Paley, William 22
parables 56–58, 141–143, 147–149, 191–193, 213, 231, 276–277, 302–303, 330
Paradise Lost 20
Pascal, Blaise 221–222, 226, 314
Passion 176

Pasteur, Louis 311–313
patience 157–162
Paul, St. 28–29, 39, 85, 95, 100, 112, 120, 159, 179, 180, 181, 229–230, 263–265, 267–268, 296, 327–328, 340–341, 347, 357–358
Paul VI, Pope 356
peace 361–373
Penn, William 160, 171, 325, 372
Pentecost 92, 98–99
Pentecostalism 101–102
Peter, St. 150, 179, 180, 255–256
Philarete of Moscow, St. 87
Philip Neri, St. 277
Pilgrim Fathers 351–353
pilgrimage 353–354
Pius IX, Pope 285
Plagues of Egypt 245–247
Pollock, Robert 286
Porete, Marguerite 42
Possenti, Gabriel 45
posterity 311–315
prayer 51, 227–238
Prodigal Son 302–303
prophets 35, 87, 88, 200–208
prudence 190–197
Pseudo-Dionysius the Areopagite 36, 70–71, 235

Puls, Sister Joan 153
Punshon, William Morley 321

Quakers 371–372
Quarles, Francis 350

Rabbula of Edessa 149
Raleigh, Sir Walter 355
Raphael 73
reconciliation 138–145
Redemption 119
repentance 146–156
resurrection 63, 64, 65, 207
Ridler, Anne 283
Roger of Taizé, Brother 328
Rolle, Richard 44, 103
Rose of Lima, St. 99
Rossetti, Christina 160, 323
Rowley, H.H. 201–202
Rowntree, John Wilhelm 36
Ruskin, John 279
Ruysbroeck, Jan van 63

saints, making of 159, 180–181
Salesian Society 74
salvation 95–96
Samael 73
Samson 82
Satan 20, 24, 73, 78, 79, 258
Saunders, Dame Cicely 128
Schleiermacher, Friedrich 34
Schweitzer, Albert 318, 354
Sea of Galilee 245

seraphs 71
Sermon on the Mount 210, 341
Serpent 24, 27–28
silence 45
Siloam, Pool of 247
Simeon, Charles 153
sin 28, 95, 110, 111, 140, 144, 149, 156
Society of Friends 371–372
Solomon, King 131–132
Southwell, Robert 288
speaking in tongues 101–102
Spencer, Herbert 314
Spiritual Canticle, The 43
Stephen, St. 181
Stevenson, Robert Louis 105, 173–174, 189
stigmata 46–47
Stowe, Harriet Beecher 75
Summa Theologiae 34
Swift, Jonathan 14, 135

Taylor, Jeremy 300
Temple, William 170, 344
Ten Commandments 108–117, 212, 334
Teresa, Mother 127, 170, 276, 366, 373
Teresa of Avila, St. 7, 38, 161, 169, 180, 224, 230, 280, 286, 335
Teresa of Lisieux, St. 53–54, 59, 220, 230

Theodore of Mopsuetia 78–79
Theophilus of Antioch, St. 26–27
Thielicke, Helmut 54
Thomas the apostle 256, 257
Tillich, Paul 178
Tolstoy, Leo 118, 224
Tourville, Henri de 217, 309
Tower of Babel 32, 249
Transfiguration 40–41
travel 350–360
truth 129–137
Tyndale, William 298

Underhill, Evelyn 223
Urban V, Pope 369
Uriel 73

Varah, Reverend Chad 330
Vaughan, Henry 52–53
Vénard, Théophane 275
Viannes, Jean 337
Vincent de Paul, St. 166, 190
Virgin Mary 45, 80, 82, 83, 285, 286, 287
    "Hail Mary" prayer 238
Visitation 82

Warfield, Benjamin 250
watchfulness 184
Watson, David 116
Watson, Thomas 226
Wedding at Cana 299

Wesley, Charles 222
Wesley, John 183, 231, 235, 251, 336, 344
Whittier, John 368
Wilberforce, William 270–271, 333–334
Williams, Harry 146
wisdom 129–137
Wise Men (Magi) 36–37, 130, 290
Wittgenstein, Ludwig 115
Word, The 85–93
Wordsworth, William 50–51, 194, 285
working together 339–349
Wyon, Olive 275

Zadkiel 73
Zeller, Hubert van 296
Zwingli, Ulrich 104

ACKNOWLEDGMENTS

The publishers wish to thank the following for their kind permission to reproduce the copyright material in this book. Every effort has been made to trace copyright holders, but if anyone has been omitted we apologize, and will, if informed, make corrections in any future edition.

Page 17: pearl 10, from *Miracles* by C.S. Lewis © C.S. Lewis Pte Ltd; **34:** pearl 54, from *New Seeds of Contemplation* by Thomas Merton, New Directions, New York, 1961; **34:** pearl 56, from Henry Havelock Ellis, *Impressions and Comments*, Constable & Company, London, 3 volumes (1914–1923); **37:** pearl 64, from *The Present Christ* by John Main, Darton Longman and Todd, London, 1995; **41:** pearl 70, © William Barclay Lectureship Trust; **42:** pearl 73, attributed to M.K. Gandhi, precise source unknown; **62:** pearl 122, from *Letters to Malcolm: Chiefly on Prayer* by C.S. Lewis © C.S. Lewis Pte Ltd; **64:** pearl 128, from *A Grief Observed* by C.S. Lewis © C.S. Lewis Pte Ltd; **65:** pearl 130, from *Does God Exist? An answer for today* by Hans Kung. English translation by Edward Quinn, ©1980, William Collins, courtesy HarperCollins, London; **93:** pearl 201, from *The Narrow Path* by Dietrich Bonhoeffer, Darton Longman and Todd, London, 1990; **100:** pearl 217 from the play *The Great God Brown* by Eugene O'Neill, William Cape, London and Boni & Liveright, New York, 1926; **127:** pearl 307, from Erich Fromm's *The Art of Loving*, Continuum International Publishing Group; Centennial edition, April 2000; **143:** pearl 354, from a poetry collection *In the Clearing* by Robert Lee Frost, Holt, Rinehart & Winston, New York and London, 1962, courtesy Henry Holt, New York; **144:** pearl 359, from the section "Love Thy Enemy" in Corrie Ten Boom, *Tramp for the Lord*, Christian Literature Crusade, 1974; **153:** pearl 383, courtesy of Sister Joan Puls, former President of the School Sisters of Saint Francis; **154:** pearl 384, from Ursula Niebuhr, reproduced by permission of John Hunt Publishing Ltd, Alresford, UK; **156:** pearl 392, from *Letters to Malcolm: Chiefly on Prayer* by C.S. Lewis © C.S. Lewis Pte Ltd; **170:** pearl 438, from William Temple, *Christ in His Church*, Macmillan & Co., London,1925, reproduced with permission of Palgrave Macmillan; **171:** pearl 443, courtesy C.S. Lewis Pte Ltd; **172–173:** pearl 448, from *Original Blessing* by Matthew Fox, Jeremy P. Tarcher/Penguin Putnam, New York, 2000; **178:** pearl 460, from *The Courage to Be* by Paul Tillich, Nisbet & Co., London, 1952; **182:** pearl 473, cited in *The Essential Reinhold Niebuhr: Selected Essays and Addresses*, Reinhold Niebuhr, edited by Robert McAfee Brown, page 251, Yale University Press, 1987; **183:** pearl 478, from *Letters and Papers from Prison* by Dietrich Bonhoeffer, translated by R.H. Fuller, first published in English by SCM Press, Canterbury,1953; **186:** pearl 484, from *Letters* (entry for 18 July 1957) by C.S. Lewis © C.S.

Lewis Pte Ltd; **201–202:** pearl 521, from *Dictionary of Bible Themes* by Harold Henry Rowley, Thomas Nelson & Sons, London, 1968, reproduced courtesy of Nelson Thornes Ltd, Cheltenham; **204–205:** pearl 531, from J.L. McKenzie, *Dictionary of the Bible*, Macmillan, London, 1965; **221:** pearl 592, from *Freedom and the Spirit* by Nikolai Berdyaev, translated by Oliver Fielding Clarke, Geoffrey Bles, London, 1935; **223:** pearl 597, from Karl Barth, *The Epistle to the Romans*, translated from the sixth edition by Edwyn C. Hoskyns, London and New York: Oxford University Press, 1968, p.39; **224:** pearl 602, from *Letters and Papers from Prison* by Dietrich Bonhoeffer, translated by R.H. Fuller, first published in English by SCM Press, Canterbury,1953; **245:** pearl 666, from *Answer to Job* by Carl Gustav Jung, translated by R.F.C. Hull, Routledge & Kegan Paul, London, 1954 (first published as "Antwort auf Hiob", Zürich, 1952); 285: pearl 00 courtesy of the Diocese of Westminster, London; **260:** pearl 705, from *Letters to an American Lady* by C.S. Lewis © C.S. Lewis Pte Ltd; **269:** pearl 729, from *New Seeds of Contemplation* by Thomas Merton, New Directions, New York, 1961; **277:** pearl 751, from *North of Boston* (chapter 3, "The Death of the Hired Man," lines 122–126) by Robert Lee Frost, New York: Henry Holt, 1915; **280:** pearl 764, from *Four Quartets* by T.S. Eliot, originally published as a single volume in 1943, reproduced courtesy Faber & Faber, London; **282–283:** pearl 773, from the poem "Christmas and Common Birth" by Anne Ridler, in Collected Poems, Carcanet, Manchester, 1994, **287:** pearl 786, writer Paul Johnson in *The Spectator* magazine, Christmas 2007 double issue – an interview on belief in the Incarnation; **292:** pearl 795, from the Church of England's *Book of Common Prayer*, the rights in which are vested in the Crown, reproduced by permission of the Crown's Patentee, Cambridge University Press; **295:** pearl 802, from the Church of England's *Book of Common Prayer*, the rights in which are vested in the Crown, reproduced by permission of the Crown's Patentee, Cambridge University Press; **296:** pearl 804, from Hubert Van Zeller as quoted in *The Macmillan Dictionary of Religious Quotations*, edited by Margaret Pepper, Macmillan, London, 1996, p.283; **302:** pearl 821, from Josh McDowell, reproduced by permission of John Hunt Publishing Ltd, Alresford, UK; **310:** pearl 843, from *Endangered – Your Child in a Hostile World* by Johann Christoph Arnold, courtesy of The Bruderhof Foundation, Farmington, Pennsylvania and Plough Publishing House,

Robertsbridge, East Sussex, 2000; **318:** pearl 859, from an address—"Monastic Dialogue and East-West Dialogue"—delivered by Thomas Merton in Calcutta in October 1968; **344:** pearl 925, from *Christianity and Social Order* by William Temple, Penguin Books, Harmondsworth and New York, 1942; **354:** pearl 949, from *Memories of Childhood and Youth* by Albert Schweitzer, translated by Charles Thomas Campion, George Allen & Unwin, London, 1924, reproduced courtesy HarperCollins Publishers Ltd, London; **362:** pearl 965, from a speech attributed to General Omar N. Bradley, Chief of Staff, United States Army, given in Boston on November 10th, 1948; **364:** pearl 971, from *Four Quartets* by T.S. Eliot, originally published as a single volume in 1943, reproduced courtesy Faber & Faber, London; **366:** pearl 977, from a public acceptance speech given in 1979 by Mother Teresa of Calcutta upon receipt of the Nobel prize; **369:** pearl 988, from the Church of England's *Book of Common Prayer*, the rights in which are vested in the Crown, reproduced by permission of the Crown's Patentee, Cambridge University Press.

ABOUT THE AUTHOR

Malcolm Day is a writer, editor, and theologian. He is the author of *A Treasury of Saints* (2002), *The Book of Miracles* (2006), and *Great Events of Bible Times* (1994).